PELICAN BOOKS

THE DEAD SEA SCROLLS

John Marco Allegro was born in London in 1923 and began his linguistic studies after war-time service in the Royal Navy. He studied at the University of Manchester, where he obtained a first-class Honours degree in Oriental Studies in 1951. The next year he was awarded the degree of M.A. for a thesis on the linguistic background of the Balaam Oracles, and was engaged on further research at Oxford on Hebrew dialects when he was asked to join the international Scrolls editing team in Jerusalem as their first British representative. He has returned to Jordan many times since then, not only to continue this work but to organize and lead a number of archaeological expeditions into the Wilderness of Judea under the auspices of the Dead Sea Scrolls Fund, of which he was Secretary and a trustee. In 1961, H.M. King Hussein appointed him Honorary adviser on the Scrolls to the Jordan Government. Besides his first publication of a number of Qumran documents, he has written several articles on Semitic philology in British and foreign periodicals, and has lectured widely on the Scrolls and broadcast frequently on sound and television on this and other subjects. His other books are *The People of the Dead Sea Scrolls* (1958), *The Treasure of the Copper Scroll* (1960), *Search in the Desert* (1964), *The Shapira Affair* (1964), *Discoveries in the Judaean Desert, V* (1967), *The Sacred Mushroom and the Cross* (1970), *The End of a Road* (1970), *The Chosen People* (1971), *Lost Gods* (1977), *The Dead Sea Scrolls and the Christian Myth* (1979), *All Manner of Men* (1982) and *Physician, Heal Thyself . . .* (1985). Until 1970 he held the post of Lecturer in Old Testament and Intertestamental Studies in the University of Manchester, and now researches and writes full-time.

JOHN ALLEGRO

The Dead Sea Scrolls

A REAPPRAISAL

with 24 plates

PENGUIN BOOKS

Penguin Books Ltd, Harmondsworth, Middlesex, England
Viking Penguin Inc., 40 West 23rd Street, New York, New York 10010, U.S.A.
Penguin Books Australia Ltd, Ringwood, Victoria, Australia
Penguin Books Canada Ltd, 2801 John Street, Markham, Ontario, Canada L3R 1B4
Penguin Books (N.Z.) Ltd, 182–190 Wairau Road, Auckland 10, New Zealand

—

First published 1956
Reprinted 1956, 1957
Reprinted with revisions, 1958, 1959
Reprinted 1961
Second edition 1964
Reprinted 1966, 1968, 1971, 1972, 1974, 1975, 1977
1978, 1980, 1982, 1984, 1986, 1987

—

—

Made and printed in Great Britain by
Richard Clay Ltd, Bungay, Suffolk
Set in Monotype Baskerville

FOR JOAN

CONTENTS

Jericho

Jerusalem

Kh. Qumran

Al Mird

'Ain Feshkha

Deir
Mar Saba

Bethlehem

Herodium

Ta'amireh Darajeh

Murabba'at

Machaerus

Hebron

DEAD

En Geddi

SEA

Masada

0 ———— 10
Miles

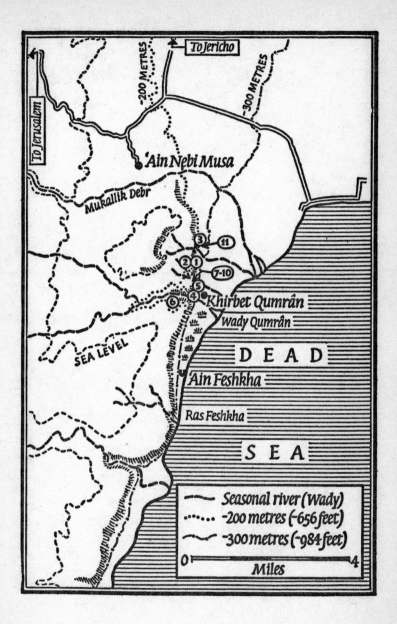

To Jericho

To Jerusalem

-200 METRES

-300 METRES

'Ain Nebi Musa

Mukallik Debr

③

⑪

②①

7-10

⑤

⑥ ④ Khirbet Qumrân

Wady Qumrân

D E A D

SEA LEVEL

'Ain Feshkha

Ras Feshkha

S E A

	Seasonal river (Wady)
	-200 metres (-656 feet)
	-300 metres (-984 feet)

0   Miles   4

PREFACE TO THE FIRST EDITION

THE following chapters make no claim to being an exhaustive study of this fabulous documentary and archaeological material from the Dead Sea; such would be quite outside the scope of a concise, popular volume. It does attempt to give to the general public some conception of the extent and importance of recent discoveries in this area, and I hope in a perspective made possible by a study of the published and unpublished material alike.

Personal acknowledgements must begin with an expression of gratitude to Mr Gerald Lankester Harding for first inviting me to take part in the editing of the Scrolls, and to Mr Harding's successors in the post of Jordanian Director of Antiquities for their unfailing courtesy in continuing to afford me every facility for studying the material and organizing archaeological expeditions in Jordan.

To Mr Joseph Saad, Curator of the Palestine Archaeological Museum in Jerusalem, I am greatly indebted for much 'inside information' on the early stages of the tracing and purchase of the Scroll fragments, and to my colleagues in the 'Scrollery' for much kind advice, although it must be stated that responsibility for opinions expressed in these pages is entirely my own.

The Curator and Trustees of the Palestine Archaeological Museum were very kind in permitting me to photograph in the Museum.

My wife Joan has helped greatly in the production of this book, not only with proof-reading and other forms of clerical assistance, but by her ready assumption of our joint domestic responsibilities during my frequent trips abroad.

PREFACE TO THE SECOND EDITION

THIS new edition of my book has given me a chance of bringing it up to date more effectively than previous reprints have permitted. Much has happened in the Scrolls field since 1956, the date of the original publication of *The Dead Sea Scrolls*. More of the fragmentary material from the Qumran and Murabba'at caves has appeared in definitive form, although the mass of material from the Fourth Cave has still to be published. I have myself tried to counter this regrettable delay by publishing the most important of the documents committed to my care in provisional form in learned journals, but specialists will still find translations in the following pages of which the Hebrew texts remain as yet unpublished. I apologize for any inconvenience caused in this respect.

There has been recently a comparative lull in the spate of articles and books on the Scrolls, and this is by no means a bad thing. Few of the publications had much original to offer, and too many of the popular works were simply rather naïve attempts on the part of Christian apologists to counter what they feared were attempts to undermine the faith of believers. One would like to think that now such effort might with more profit be directed towards a real, and if possible, objective assessment of the importance of the Dead Sea Scrolls for a clearer understanding of Christian origins. Of course, an immense amount of work has been done in this direction, and my own debt to such scholarship, which I gladly acknowledge, will be evident in the following pages. But it is pathetic that sixteen years after the first discovery of the Scrolls, scholars of the calibre of W. F. Albright and D. N. Freedman should have to deplore the fact that 'there is still a partial boycott of the Dead Sea Scrolls on the part of New Testament scholars . . .' They go on to emphasize the importance of this new field of knowledge in these words:

. . . in the Scrolls we have for the first time a direct Jewish background of the New Testament. Hitherto we have been partly dependent upon intertestamental literature (Apocrypha and Pseudepigrapha) and partly on early rabbinic literature, which is, unfortunately, a century or two later than the deeds and words of Christ and the apostles. Thanks to the

Dead Sea Scrolls, we now have direct evidence that is of the greatest significance and which bears on all our New Testament books. ('The Continuing Revolution in Biblical Research' in *Journal of Bible and Religion*, XXXI, April, 1963.)

What is perhaps even more disturbing than this 'partial boy-cott' of the Scrolls on the part of Christian scholars is the cloak of secrecy that has hung over the acquisition and disposal of these vital and often most controversial documents since 1956. Scrolls have been secretly unearthed by the Bedouin, fleetingly glimpsed by specialists, and then allowed to 'disappear' off the face of the earth. Even when others from the same cache have early on been rescued by the prompt action of the Jordanian Department of Antiquities, they have lain hidden away in the vaults of a foreign-controlled museum for several years, and only the vaguest infor-mation on their contents has been allowed to reach the outside world. When publication is eventually allowed by the trustees, it is on the extraordinary basis of 'selling' those rights for vast sums of money to foreign institutions. Meanwhile attempts are made to dissuade visiting archaeologists from joining expeditions to search systematically for more Scroll caves, and the curator of the museum comes to Britain to tell television audiences that such searches are best left to the illicit excavations of the Bedouin who, presumably, can be relied upon to channel their discoveries through the museum for rich rewards.

Some light has, however, recently penetrated the gloom of this appalling situation. There is now in existence a charitable founda-tion in this country through which public interest in practicable form can be directed for the finding, preservation, and publication of the Scrolls. The trustees of this Dead Sea Scrolls Fund, of which I am one, have no axe to grind, religious or academic. Our sole interest is to ensure that the full potentialities of this 'miracle of the Scrolls' may be realized and that such a bridge may be built between the antagonistic faiths of this world that no amount of religious bigotry and intolerance shall again divide the peoples of mankind. Already the Fund has sponsored a number of small expeditions in the Judaean Wilderness and has found a most willing supporter in His Majesty King Hussein and his govern-ment. Through their help these deserts have been opened up to the archaeologist as never before. The way is open to a thorough ex-ploration of possible Scroll sites on a systematic basis. Everything now depends on the financial support we may expect from home, and in the hope of promoting such assistance, I am glad to offer the public this revised edition of my little book.

Prestbury, Cheshire   JOHN ALLEGRO
November 1963.

CHAPTER ONE

THE DISCOVERY AND PURCHASE
OF THE SCROLLS

THE dust had hardly settled over the battlefields of the
world, when newspapers began to carry reports of a sensa-
tional new discovery in the field of biblical archaeology. It
was announced that, in the summer of 1947, a cave had
been found near the Dead Sea which had produced manuscripts of the book of Isaiah older by something like a
thousand years than any previously known Hebrew copy
of the Old Testament. Later examination was to show that,
of the scrolls found in this cave, the biblical manuscripts
were probably the least important of what appeared to be
the remains of a Jewish sectarian library dating from
shortly after the time of Jesus Christ. More discoveries in
this region followed in the ensuing years, and before long
the world was in possession of the remains of hundreds of
scrolls covering a period which had hitherto been one of the
most sparsely documented, yet important, periods in man's
history. Questions which had been hammering at the door
of scholarship since the beginning of critical research into
Christian origins could now be answered. In this book I
have attempted to trace the general outline of results so far
achieved and where further research may be expected to
lead as this exciting new material becomes generally available. But first let us see how the discovery was made, and to
do so we must travel to the wilderness of Judaea, to a point
amongst the mountains bordering the Dead Sea, a few
miles south of Jericho.

Muhammad Adh-Dhib had lost a goat. The lad was a
member of the Ta'amireh tribe of semi-Bedouin who range
the wilderness between Bethlehem and the Dead Sea (see
map on p. 8), and he had been out all this summer's day

tending the animals entrusted to his care. Now one of them had wandered, skipping into the craggy rocks above. Muhammad pulled himself wearily up the limestone cliffs, calling the animal as it went higher and higher in search of food. The sun became hotter, and finally the lad threw himself into the shade of an overhanging crag to rest a while. His eye wandered listlessly over the glaring rocks and was suddenly arrested by a rather queerly placed hole in the cliff face, hardly larger than a man's head (pl. 1). It appeared to lead inwards to a cave, and yet was too high for an ordinary cave entrance, of which there were hundreds round about. Muhammad picked up a stone and threw it through the hole, listening for the sound as it struck home. What he heard brought him sharply to his feet. Instead of the expected thud against solid rock, his sharp ears had detected the metallic ring of pottery. He listened a moment, and then tried again, and again there could be no doubt that his stone had crashed among potsherds. A little fearfully the Bedouin youth pulled himself up to the hole, and peered in. His eyes were hardly becoming used to the gloom when he had to let himself drop to the ground. But what he had seen in those few moments made him catch his breath in amazement. On the floor of the cave, which curved back in a natural fault in the rock, there were several large, cylindrical objects standing in rows. The boy pulled himself up again to the hole, and holding on until his arms and fingers were numb, saw, more clearly this time, that they were large, wide-necked jars, with broken pieces strewn all about them. He waited no longer, but dropped to the ground and was off like a hare, his goat and flock forgotten in a frantic desire to put as much distance between himself and this jinn-ridden cave as possible. For who else but a desert spirit could be living in such a place with an entrance too small for a man?

That night Muhammad discussed his discovery with a friend who, being the elder, was entitled to scoff at the superstitions of his junior. He urged Muhammad to take him to the spot, and the next day the two of them went to the cave, and this time squeezed through the hole and dropped inside. It was just as the younger lad had des-scribed. The jars stood in rows on each side of the narrow cave, and, in the middle, broken sherds lay amidst debris fallen from the roof. There were seven or eight of the jars all told, and some had large, bowl-like lids. They lifted one and peered in, but found it empty. And so with another, and another, until in the third they saw a bundle of rags and under it two more. If they had hoped for the glitter of gold and precious stones they were sorely disappointed, for the bundles crumbled at a touch, and, pulling away some of the folds, they could see only some black tarry substance and, below that, folds of smooth brown leather. When, later, the boys had taken this booty back to their camp, they took off all the wrappings from the large bundle, and unrolled the scroll it contained, until, as they later recounted wonder-ingly, it stretched from one end of the tent to the other. It seems certain that this must have been the larger of the two manuscripts of Isaiah, the news of which was to set the biblical world astir. However, at the time it evoked little interest among its new owners who could neither read the strange writing inscribed on it, nor think of anything useful to which they could put the leather, fragile as it was. So for a time the Bedouin carried the scrolls about with them as they pastured their flocks and made what trade they could with their neighbours. These Bedouin have no real home. The world is their prey and usually their enemy. This tribe had been in the vicinity since the seventeenth century, and they have managed to eke out a sparse enough living with their few animals, now and again putting their detailed knowledge of the territory to better gain in smuggling. Until the area became effectively policed by the Arab Legion, they practised highway robbery when they could, and always found a ready market for their trading, legal or illegal, in Bethlehem. It was to this town that they made regular visits to sell their milk and cheese, and there, one market day, they took the three scrolls. Their general dealer happened to be an Assyrian Christian, by name

Khalil Iskander Shahin, known locally as Kando (pl. 3a), who, besides the small general store patronized by the Ta'amireh, owned a cobbler's shop next door (pl. 3b). When the Bedouin showed him the scrolls, he evinced little interest, but thought they might serve as raw material for his cobbler's business. Later, after they had been kicking about the floor of the shop for some days, he picked one up and looked more closely at the surface. The writing was as meaningless to him as to the Bedouin, but it occurred to him that his spiritual guardians in Jerusalem might know more about it, and accordingly one day when he was going up to the city, he took the scrolls along with him, to the Syrian Convent of St Mark in the Old City. This much is certain, but it must be confessed that from here on the story begins to disintegrate, as love of truth on the part of the chief actors in the drama gives way before fear and cupidity. One thing is certain, however; Kando began to realize that the scrolls had some monetary value and found out that the Bedouin had by no means cleared the cave. He and his accomplice George accordingly launched a minor archaeological expedition to the cave indicated by the Bedouin and collected at least a number of large fragments and probably at this time the remainder of the scrolls, making seven in all. After they had taken all they could find, they seem to have let the Syrian authorities of St Mark's into the secret. In any case the Metropolitan organized his own expedition to the cave, which proceeded to ransack the place, making a large opening near the ground, and pulling out everything they could lay their hands on. Of course, it will be realized that all such excavations were and are completely illegal under the laws of the country, whether of the Mandate or of the succeeding Jordan Government. All such archaeological material remains the property of the country in which it is found, until the Government directs otherwise. So complete secrecy shrouded all these operations, and much harm was done as a result. It is certain that the Syrians found some more fragments, but valuable archaeological data like linen wrappings and sherds from the broken jars they threw on to a rubbish dump outside. Kando had meanwhile deposited the scrolls in his possession with the Metropolitan, on a security, he now says, of £24; and these, and some fragments, the Church leader began to hawk round the various scholastic institutions of Jerusalem to get an idea of their worth. It seems that one of the scrolls was shown to the late Professor E. L. Sukenik of the Hebrew University, who kept it for some time and then set about finding the rest of the scrolls, which he had realized were very old and of considerable value. He made a perilous journey to Bethlehem, for by now the Jewish–Arab hostilities had become open warfare following on the withdrawal of the Mandate. There he seems to have contacted Kando and brought away three more scrolls. This gentleman now began to get scared since he was afraid that the news of the illegal excavations would leak out, and he would rightly be held responsible by the authorities. He therefore took the precaution of burying some of the largest fragments from the cave in his garden at Bethlehem! Unfortunately, the soil of Kando's back garden is somewhat different from the parched dust of the Qumran caves, and when later he went to retrieve them he found only several lumps of sticky glue.

Meanwhile, in Jerusalem, the Syrian Metropolitan was continuing his rounds trying to discover if the scrolls were really old. Finally, on 18 February 1948 he called up the American School of Oriental Research and spoke to Dr John C. Trever, who had been left in temporary charge of the establishment during the absence of the Director. He told Trever that during a clear-out of his library at the Convent, he had found some old Hebrew manuscripts on which he would like his advice. An appointment was made for the next day, and the Metropolitan sent round the scrolls packed in an old suitcase, by the hand of a Father Butros Sowmy and his brother. After some hasty comparing of pictures of other ancient Hebrew manuscripts, and complicated research into dictionaries and concordances, Trever discovered that he was looking at a scroll of Isaiah, and that as far as he was able to tell, it was genuinely very old. He asked permission to make photographs of the scroll, and after some negotiations did so. As he worked he became more and more excited, for if it was as old as a favourable comparison with a photograph of a pre-Christian Hebrew papyrus fragment would seem to indicate, then he was handling the oldest manuscript of the Bible ever known. It was only with great difficulty that Trever could restrain his impatience when, half way through the work of photography, he had to fulfil a long-standing engagement with the Curator of the Palestine Museum, then Mr Harry Iliffe, to go to Jericho and take photographs of a local excavation. But if any mention of the discovery was made at the time to the authorities responsible for the control of antiquities in Palestine, little attention seems to have been paid to the story, and nothing was done to organize adequate and immediate steps to safeguard the treasures and seal the cave until a properly equipped expedition could probe its secrets. Trever urged the Metropolitan to take the documents out of the city, since the situation was fast deteriorating, and war was beginning to stalk the streets and hills of that unhappy land. The archaeologists themselves were obliged to leave Jerusalem, and it was not until November 1948, when the April copies of the *Bulletin of the American Schools of Oriental Research* reached Jerusalem, that Mr G. Lankester Harding, newly responsible for the archaeological interests of Arab Palestine as well as Trans-Jordan, learnt that eighteen months before, a fabulous discovery had been made by the Dead Sea. By now photographs of the scrolls had been examined by competent palaeographers such as Professor W. F. Albright and pronounced definitely pre-Christian, probably dating to the first or second centuries before our era. Excitement ran high all over the scholarly world, and in Jordan Harding was now faced with an extremely difficult and urgent problem. The source of these scrolls had to be found, and, if any related archaeological material remained, it had to be expertly examined at the first opportunity, not only to confirm the palaeographical dating but to determine the community from whose library they had come. Furthermore, it seemed not improbable that there might be more scrolls, and certainly fragments, since apparently some of the documents found were in a fragile condition with pieces missing from the outside and edges. But the original discovery had taken place so long ago that the chances of finding the source relatively free from tampering were very slight. The Metropolitan had succeeded in smuggling the scrolls in his possession out of the country, and had taken them to America. The Jordan Government, of course, demanded their immediate return, but by now the monetary values being accorded them in the popular Press were so astronomical as to persuade the Syrian Church leader that the chances of his returning were well worth sacrificing for the sake of the money he could expect to raise in their sale. The one bright light in the whole miserable affair at this stage was that he had agreed with Trever and the American Schools to allow them to photograph and publish the scrolls immediately, whilst their sale was being negotiated. The Americans had told him that if they were published quickly their value would be much enhanced. In fact, momentarily, it declined, since once they were readily available in printed form the need for the originals became less urgent. The American scholars did, in fact, publish them, extraordinarily well and quickly, putting the scholarly world greatly in their debt.

Back in Jordan, Harding had gone immediately to the Palestine Archaeological Museum in Jerusalem, and in his capacity as Acting Curator instructed Joseph Saad (pl. 2b), the new Secretary, to spare no effort in discovering the whereabouts of the fabulous cave and any other information he could about the find and the personalities involved. Saad's first call was to the American School, and there Dr O. R. Sellers, that year's Director, immediately offered all the help in his power. Together they went to St Mark's Monastery, despite the extremely dangerous nature of the journey through the Old City, where Jewish shells and sniping were making it near suicide to be out of doors during daylight.

Slipping from shelter to shelter they finally arrived at the building which backs on to the dividing wall between Arab and Jewish Jerusalem, and there interviewed a person by the name of George Isaiah. It became clear from the beginning that he was not going to be very helpful, and, although he did not deny that the Monastery had organized an excavation of the cave, refused point-blank to disclose its whereabouts. Saad argued, cajoled, and bullied, but all to no effect, and he was just about to give up hope of gaining any useful information at all when, out of the corner of his eye, he saw one of the Syrian fathers approaching, a venerable saint called Father Yusif. When the old man had drawn quite near, Saad suddenly turned from George and asked Yusif what he knew about the cave. Before George could stop him, the old man began to describe the excavations and their whereabouts. George turned on him fiercely, but could not silence him before he had given at least a general idea of the cave's position. It seemed that it was somewhere south of the junction of the roads to Jericho and the Dead Sea, amongst the cliffs which border the Sea to the west. Now those limestone cliffs are honeycombed with caves and clefts in the rock, and the mountains rise nearly a thousand feet from the marly plateau, so that with a southern limit at Ras Feshkha about six miles to the south, a good deal more detailed pin-pointing was going to be necessary for the cave to be discovered (see map on p. 9). As Saad and his companion retraced their steps through the Old City, they discussed the next move. It seemed obvious that they would have to try the great standby of the East, bribery. Most things out there have their price, and it only remained to find out how high it was going to be. So, on their return, negotiations with George Isaiah were opened, on the general principle that, if he would lead a party to the cave, he would receive a cash payment, and the custody of any further scrolls found would be equally shared between them. These negotiations took a considerable time, involving many trips to the Monastery through gun-fire. Finally, when it seemed that arrangements were sufficiently far advanced,

Saad arranged for the mayor of Jerusalem and his digni-
taries to accompany them to St Mark's to witness the formal
agreement. The party arrived on the day appointed and
took their seats. Everybody asked after everybody else's
health, and were asked in return, and Allah duly thanked.
Coffee was passed round, and, after that, the customary
small talk ensued, without which no Arab meeting is considered opened. Sellers was beginning to get restless, but
Saad, raised in the traditions of the East, played the game
in all its formality and was patient. At last, after the seventh
round of thanking Allah for their individual good health,
the main subject was broached, the terms stated, and nothing but the clasping of hands remained to seal the bargain.
And George Isaiah would have nothing to do with it.

Sellers and Joseph parted gloomily at the gates of the
American School, and Saad carried on to the Museum.
Weeks of negotiation had produced practically nothing
and, apart from its general locality, they knew little more
about the cave than what had been learnt from the American
Bulletin. Now it happened that the Museum at this time
was in the hands of the Arab Legion, and Saad had to pass
a ring of sentries to reach his quarters. He made a per-
functory greeting to the man on duty at the gate and then
something prompted him to hesitate and look at the soldier
more closely. He was a lean, dark-skinned Arab of the
desert, of the type Glubb always chose for his picked
troops, and Saad studied his face for a moment, noticing
his long, straight, Semitic nose, his short curly beard, and
black smouldering eyes. He was a true son of the desert
from the sandy wastes of the Hijaz, trained from his boy-
hood in desert lore and with eyes as keen as an eagle's. It
occurred to Saad that if anybody could find that cave,
given general directions as to its whereabouts, men like this
soldier could. They would be able to perceive from an
amazing distance any disturbance of the ground round the
illicit excavations, and so detect the cave perhaps even from
ground level. The idea crystallized into a plan of campaign;
and, waiting only to collect Sellers from the American

School, Saad went in search of the officer in charge of the troops in the Jerusalem area, a Major-General Lash. He found this officer well prepared, for only a night or two before he had been discussing the problem with a Belgian United Nations observer, Captain Lippens, and had that day telephoned to Harding in Amman, asking if he would like him to send a few of his desert troops down to the area to search for the caves. Harding had agreed; and now, with the added information Saad was able to provide, no further time was lost and a detachment of troops under the direction of an English officer, Brigadier Ashton, and a Jordanian, Captain (now Major) Akkash el Zebn, was sent down to the road junction by the Dead Sea. Deploying from this point, in such a way that as far as possible no section of the cliffs at all visible from the littoral plain would miss their scrutiny, they set off slowly, working their way south. Within seventy-two hours, Akkash was on the phone reporting that they had found the cave, and asking for further instructions. Whilst waiting for Harding's arrival, Ashton plotted the cave and started collecting the pottery which lay round about, making accurate notes and drawings which were of the greatest help to the excavators later. Then Harding arrived, and together they made the first preliminary excavation. Harding confesses that when he first saw the cave he was dubious of its being the source of the scrolls, but the presence of undoubtedly ancient pottery made it worth investigating further. He asked Ashton to mount a guard on the cave until such time as a properly equipped archaeological party could be assembled. This was done, but the expedition was dogged by bad luck for days. Every time they gathered at the road junction it rained, which made the tracks completely impassable to their transport, and once it even snowed! Ashton could not leave his men standing about outside a cave by the Dead Sea for long, however, and it became urgent to mount the expedition, which finally started work on 15 February 1949, a fortnight after the rediscovery of the cave. Father De Vaux of the French School of Archaeology, Joseph Saad, and two others joined the excavation, and the early finding of scores of small inscribed fragments of leather, together with pieces of the linen wrappings (pl. 5b), and the sherds of dozens of the characteristic large scroll jars, in which it was said that the original scrolls had been found, soon made it plain that this was certainly a scroll cave, if not the original one. The damage caused by illegal excavations was all too plain; no hope could now be entertained of any stratification of the remains, and some of the most valuable of the pottery and wrappings had been tossed outside on to a dump. The number of jars originally placed in the cave was now seen to have been between forty and fifty, and if, as it was then thought, each of those jars had held several scrolls, then it became a matter of extreme urgency to find the rest which might still be in the country and perhaps suffering damage. In any case, there must clearly have been hundreds of fragments, and these had also to be found and studied together if they were to be of any use at all.

Another detective inquiry was instituted, and Saad given *carte blanche* to find and, if necessary, buy those pieces regardless of cost. It was clear now, as more and more reports came in from scholars studying the first scrolls, that every word of these documents was going to be worth its weight in gold; and, indeed, that was just about what they were going to cost before they were all finally in safe hands.

Saad went again to the Monastery of St Mark's, this time accompanied by Harding himself. The object of this inquiry was to find out the name of the dealer in Bethlehem who had continually cropped up in reports, but had never been named. If there were more scrolls and fragments about, he was the most likely person to know about them, and he would also know the names and tribe of the Bedouin who had found the cave. George Isaiah was a little more informative this time, but could not or would not describe the cave in sufficient detail to make its identification with the Legion's discovery certain, and refused to disclose the name of the dealer. Saad knew better this time than to waste much time over him. After the inevitable coffee, and inquiries after each other's health, with no more useful information forthcoming, they rose to leave, keeping their eyes open all the time for Father Yusif. It was as they were leaving the gate of the Monastery that they saw the frail figure approaching, and immediately engaged him in conversation on the cave. Unfortunately, they now seemed to know more than he, and still they lacked the name of the Bethlehem dealer. Then they had an amazing piece of luck. Harding had noticed that as they had been speaking to Father Yusif, a woman across the road had been showing keen interest in their conversation. Finally, she came across to them and spoke. Were they talking about the excavations of the Dead Sea cave which George Isaiah had organized about a year ago? Her husband had taken part in the 'dig', and had even been rewarded for his pains with a leather fragment, which the priests had told him was most valuable, although he had not yet discovered a way of converting it into hard cash. However, if they would like to wait a moment she would see if she could find him; he could not be far away. Saad and Harding looked at each other, and then to heaven. They finally ran the man, Jabra by name, to earth in a nearby coffee shop, and induced him to come along to the Museum. In the basement, the spoils of the official excavation of the cave were arranged on large trestle tables, and, bringing him near, Harding asked Jabra if he could see anything there that he recognized. The man looked long and earnestly over the table, and then a broad smile lit his face. Yes, this. Amidst the broken pottery and linen wrappings, the Roman lamp and the cooking pot, he had spied his own dear, long-lost but never forgotten cigarette roller. So another link in the chain was forged, the cave was now definitely identified, and it now remained to find out how much more Jabra knew. An Arab who realizes that he has partaken, however unwittingly, in an illegal act, is a wary creature. Harding and Saad had somehow to win his confidence, if they were to obtain the information they so desperately wanted. Bribery was of course inevitable, and a generous tip went far towards loosening Jabra's tongue. He admitted that they had found some scroll fragments and that the Metropolitan had taken most of them away with him when he left. They tackled him about the name of the Bethlehem dealer; but at once he shut up like a clam, and for a long time would say nothing on the subject. Harding saw the fear of death in his eyes, and the man confessed that he was literally scared for his life. It took a great deal of alternate threatening and re-assuring before they finally forced the truth from him; and, when they had let him scurry off home, Saad and Harding sat down and faced one another. Events now had taken a sinister turn. If Jabra's fears were justified, it meant that this dealer and his confederates were willing to go to any length to avoid interference in their territory. It was clear that from now on the game would be played to very high stakes, perhaps to higher values than mere money.

The journey to Bethlehem was an adventure in itself. Today it takes only half an hour of smooth driving on a new tarmac road to go from Jerusalem to Bethlehem, and before the troubles a more direct road took only half that time. In 1949, with this in Jewish hands, as it still is, the makeshift route was long and dangerous, a dirt track which snaked far out into the Judaean hills by the monastery of Mar Saba. Transport was by donkey, and the journey took half a day. The morning following the interview with Jabra, Saad set out, taking with him two of the Museum guards, and reached Bethlehem shortly after midday. Leaving the guards and the animals on the outskirts of the town, he walked into the centre, feeling suddenly lonely and unprotected. From now on he would be working alone; any sign of official support, and every way would be blocked; the dealer, scrolls, and everything else would go underground and nothing ever recovered. But Bethlehem in those days, cut off from a central government by the fighting, was no place for an unprotected man to face a gang of desperate brigands, and Joseph hesitated a moment outside the shop which had been pointed out to him as Kando's (pl. 3b). It opened, like all such eastern shops, straight on to the street, and behind the piles of vegetables and hanging kuffiyas, the bright sunlight did not penetrate. Joseph peered into the shadows but could see nothing from outside. Then he entered.

His eyes took a little time to accustom themselves to the gloom, so he did not at first see the men standing at the back of the room, watching him. One of them was rather portly, heavy-jowled, and dressed in the long Arab nightshirt type of garment, with a red tarbush on his head. His companion was an older man who stared at Joseph suspiciously from beneath heavy eyebrows, and glanced from time to time at his companion and the door standing ajar behind him. Saad realized from their manner that news of his arrival had preceded him and came straight to the point. He had heard that Kando knew something about the scrolls which had been found in a cave, and furthermore, had some of the illegally excavated fragments in his possession. There was a moment's heavy silence, and then the old man flew at him, calling him a government spy, traitor, and worse, pushing Saad against the wall as he hurled abuse at him. Joseph raised his arms to fend off his assailant, but, even as he did so, saw the other man slip out of the open door and shut it behind him. Almost immediately the old man calmed down, glancing behind him to ensure that Kando had got clear, but Saad knew now that there was nothing to be gained by waiting longer and left the shop to return to his friends. Now the fat was really in the fire. Kando knew what he was after and suspected him of being in league with the Government. The chances were that he would either try to silence Saad, or smuggle the incriminating evidence out of the country and make off until things had quietened down. The safest thing for Saad to do would have been to make tracks for Jerusalem and his well-guarded Museum. Instead he sent his men away, and took lodgings in Bethlehem, determined to try and win his way into Kando's confidence. It was the act of a brave man.

Day after day Joseph returned to the little shop, engaging Kando in conversation at first on anything but the scrolls. He made the acquaintance of George, who appeared to be

Kando's right-hand man and had certainly cooperated with him in the illicit digging. Slowly he won their confidence, and one day brought up the subject of the scrolls again. He hastened to reassure them that no ill would come to them from working with him; indeed, if they would trust him he would find them a market for their fragments which would pay well and be perfectly safe. After all, if they tried to smuggle them out of the country they might lose everything, including their freedom. They would lose nothing doing things Saad's way. The logic of Joseph's reasoning gradually had its effect, and the first suspicion gave way to a wary, but nevertheless, genuine friendship. When he finally left Bethlehem, it was with a promise from Kando that he would come and visit him at the Museum. On the journey back, Joseph reflected rather ruefully that he had not seen a single fragment during all those days in Bethlehem; yet, on balance, he was not displeased with progress.

Kando kept his word and soon after appeared at Jerusalem, and Saad in due course paid a return visit. This went on for some weeks without further mention being made of the fragments, and Joseph was almost beginning to wonder if Kando had already sold them or, indeed, had ever possessed any. Then one day, in the gardens of the Museum, Kando took Saad over to a shady corner, looked at him hard, and then thrust his hand into the grimy 'nightshirt' and brought out a wallet. Inside, as he slowly opened it, there lay a piece of inscribed parchment, about the size of three or four fingers. Saad took the piece in his hand and studied it. There could be no doubt that the writing was very similar to that on the fragments he had already seen and the leather on which it was written was genuinely old. He replaced it carefully in the folds of Kando's wallet, knowing that one false move now could forfeit in a moment all the confidence he had built up over these trying weeks. Nevertheless, as he watched the wallet go back into its home, he wondered if he would ever see that precious fragment again. However, the game had to be played out the hard way; if Kando had that piece he would probably have a lot more, and Harding had told him to get the lot. Saad showed his interest in buying the piece and any more that Kando might have, and on this they parted, Joseph reporting the new development to Harding. In a few days Kando returned, ready to take negotiations further. Who was Saad acting for? Joseph answered that an English Professor visiting the country was anxious to buy these fragments, but wanted more than this one piece; how much had he to offer? Kando rather warily replied that he had 'quite a lot', and arranged a rendezvous at which Saad would bring the 'English Professor' and where Kando would have all the pieces in his possession. The place appointed was to be in Jericho; and, when the date and time had been arranged, Saad went off to find the mythical financier. It so happened that, working with Harding at this time as a non-technical assistant, was an Englishman, Mr Richmond Brown, who willingly agreed to take the part. At a preliminary meeting Harding handed over a thousand pounds in one dinar notes (1 Jordan dinar = 1 pound sterling), but told Saad to try and obtain all the fragments in Kando's possession for eight hundred pounds. The absolute maximum was fixed at a pound per square centimetre of fragment, but to try and ascribe any monetary value at all to this priceless material was extremely difficult. If this price seems outrageously high, it must be remembered that, at that time, the Syrian Metropolitan was asking something like a million dollars for the scrolls in his possession, and reports to this effect were being heard all over Jordan on the radio. The Bedouin and Kando were now well aware that these scrolls were considered beyond price by the outside world, and that their recovery was worth almost any amount of money. It should be also recognized that behind all these negotiations there lay the shadow of irresponsible people who were willing to buy illegally smuggled pieces for their collections or as souvenirs, or in order to make a profit on a further transaction. The danger of such loss was ever present forcing the pace, and thus raising the price. It was bad enough that the complete scrolls should be taken from the country, but at least they could be published as a unity, as the American scholars were doing so admirably. But with fragments, it was different. They could only be made of use to scholarship if they were kept together, and as far as possible reunited with their parent documents. A small piece of Dead Sea scroll may look very nice framed and hung over the mantel-piece, but it may well ruin the value of other larger pieces, depending for their sense on the inscription on the 'sou-venir'. Furthermore, irresponsibility is not the sole pre-rogative of tourists and dealers. At a later stage, one world-famous museum was willing to consider buying fragments smuggled from Jordan in order to have them in their cases, even though to have taken them would have delayed the publication of thousands of others, or, at least, reduced their value for want of the additional evidence. Happily the possibility was then foiled by the more responsible attitude of an Eastern University who procured the fragments and returned them immediately to Jordan. Thus at this stage there was little quibbling about price; the main thing was to rescue the fragments and give them to the world in as complete a form and as soon as possible.

Kando's choice in hotels ran pretty low. This was a dirty, fifth-rate hovel, and, as the two drew near, Saad could see that Kando was fearing a trap and taking no chances. Lounging on both sides of the street and round the entrance were some of the grimmest, toughest-looking characters one could wish not to meet anywhere, and they watched Saad and his companion through every move and gesture as they approached. Joseph felt the thick wad of notes bulging in his pocket, and thought they could not have been more conspicuous if he had carried them in his hand. The hairs on their necks bristled as they walked through the porch, trying to look unconcerned. Casually they asked a shifty-looking proprietor if Kando was there, and he motioned them to a room leading off the main entrance hall. Saad put his hands on the notes in his pocket, squared his shoulders, and the two of them walked in.

Kando was standing with George at the far side of the

room. A table covered with a greasy cloth stood in the centre, and Saad noticed that, as usual, Kando had prepared for a quick exit with a window standing wide open behind him. It idly crossed Joseph's mind to wonder if they were as well prepared. A brief greeting did nothing to relieve the tension, and Saad asked abruptly if Kando had got the fragments. The man nodded and raised his eyebrows questioningly in return. In answer, with studied carelessness, Joseph brought out the bundles of notes, stripped off the band, and fanned them out on to the table. It was a magnificent gesture and Kando hesitated no longer, but laid on to the table beside the notes a pile of decrepit-looking pieces of skin, torn and rotted at the edges, and covered with a fine white dust through which the ancient writing could just be seen. Saad passed them over to the 'English Professor' who at once began measuring them with a pocket rule. The tension had now decreased considerably, and whilst Richmond Brown was at work, Saad engaged Kando in conversation. Brown's calculations actually brought the figure to 1,250 sq. cm., but following his instructions he said 'I can only give eight hundred pounds for this lot.' Saad looked at Kando expectantly, but the latter jerked his head and gave the click of the tongue which is the Arabic refusal. Then he began to collect the fragments together, and Saad after a while did the same with the notes. Each delayed the process as long as possible, hoping for the other to give way, but when they both had finished the silence remained unbroken. Saad walked to the door, followed by Brown, both wondering if Kando would let them go through that grim circle of henchmen with a thousand pounds in their pockets. However, they passed unmolested and started to walk towards the Winter Palace Hotel where Harding awaited them. Certainly they were alive, and had handled the precious fragments, but were they to lose them all for the sake of two hundred pounds? Harding, however, having heard their story supported their action, and was sure that the next day would see Kando at the Museum with his pieces, more than willing to sell them for eight hundred pounds.

The next day sure enough, Kando appeared. But he seemed curiously certain of his ground, and would not go below a thousand pounds. Saad said he would go and ask the 'Professor' and stepped next door to where Harding sat in the Board Room, awaiting developments. Harding agreed to the price and Saad returned and gave Kando the money. Then part of the cause of his confidence became apparent, for as Kando handed him the fragments, he looked at Joseph and said, 'and give my greetings to Mr Harding'. Saad remembered then that, when the three of them had left the Winter Palace in Jericho that day, a bystander had stared curiously into the windows of the car. Of course, Kando now knew the secret of Saad's relationship with the Director of Antiquities, and probably realized that the 'English Professor' had been a fake. He knew too that the Government meant to deal leniently with him so long as he played their game. Indeed, Harding still had much to learn about the finding of that cave, and wanted badly to know the names of the Bedouin lads who had climbed through the hole. It was by no means certain that with Kando's collection all the fragment material from the cave had been exhausted, and there was always the possibility that new caves in the vicinity might be found any day, now that the Bedouin were on the look-out.

Eventually, Kando told Saad the names of the Bedouin and their tribe, and in due course they were persuaded to leave their desert camps and come to Amman. There Harding learned the full story of the discovery, and the Bedouin found a new friend in the Director of Antiquities. Well dined and liberally tipped, the lads returned to their shepherding to enliven the camp fires of their tribe with marvellous tales of the great city across the Jordan, and of an English official of their Government who spoke their tongue as well as they, and knew their customs and their lore better than any foreigner they had ever met. The wise administrator knows when to put the letter of the law into second place, and, to the fact that Harding is such a person, the world owes much of the light which further discoveries in the Judaean desert were to throw upon this important Jewish sect by the Dead Sea.

CHAPTER TWO

FURTHER DISCOVERIES

Two years later, in the autumn of 1951, some Bedouin of the Ta'amireh tribe appeared at the Jerusalem Museum bringing a piece of leather sandal and a scroll fragment the size of the palm of a hand. They told Joseph Saad that these objects had been found in another cave some distance from the first. Saad asked that they should bring with them next time the people who had actually made the discovery, so that they might lead him to the place. As he looked hard at the piece they had brought, and some of the excitement of the cave-hunt two years previously returned, Joseph wondered if they were speaking the truth in saying that this had really come from another cave. Had it, in fact, come from the first? It seemed hardly likely that it would have taken all this time to make an appearance if it had been found in 1947. But if another cave had been found, what new treasures were even now being hidden away in Bedouin saddlebags? Would the whole weary business of tracking them down and buying have to begin all over again? Perhaps this time there was a better chance of nipping the illegal excavations in the bud; yet even now it might be too late.

Saad waited anxiously throughout the next day and the next, but the Bedouin made no further appearance. De Vaux was in Europe at the time, and Harding away from Jerusalem, so whatever was to be done must be done quickly and on Saad's own initiative. First he took the fragment to a scholar at the French School to obtain another opinion on its authenticity and then went straight to his old friend Brigadier Ashton, who had proved so cooperative two years before. He asked for a Jeep and some men, with a letter of authority by which he could obtain help from any Army post in the vicinity of his search. Ashton did all this, and gave him his personal bodyguard as escort, together with a further couple of soldiers. They drove immediately to Bethlehem, and from there to the nearest Ta'amireh camp.

Saad was received with customary Bedouin hospitality, but he could feel that they were much on their guard. He tried to work the conversation around to caves and scrolls, but made no progress. When they in turn began to press him for the reason for his expedition, he replied that they were out game-shooting. They asked him where his own gun was and pressed him hard until, with sinking heart, Joseph realized that he was going to find out nothing from this camp, and would probably only antagonize them by making his questions more pointed and his own answers more evasive. In the end he pleaded tiredness and curled up on the ground to sleep.

The next morning they left the camp early, pressing on into the desert as far as their transport could take them. They soon began to realize that they were being watched. By now their presence in the area would be known throughout Ta'amireh territory. Even if they did by chance approach the cave, all work would immediately be stopped and the excavators go into hiding.

It was late in the morning when Joseph finally gave the order to return to Bethlehem. He spent the drive there hunched in his seat, trying to think of a possible move to counter the first defeat. They had reached the town almost before he knew it, and he looked up to find that they were bowling down the main street. Suddenly he clutched the driver's arm, and shouted to him to pull in to the side. An Arab padding down the road towards them had seemed strangely familiar. Then Saad recognized him as being one of the party who had come to the Museum bringing the sandal and the scroll fragment. As the Jeep slewed to a stop, Saad called the man over and immediately demanded more information about the cave. Fear came into the Arab's eyes and he made as if to move on. The soldiers leapt down from the Jeep and barred his way. Then, at a nod from Saad they lifted the man bodily and pushed him into the back of the truck. The driver let in the clutch and they roared off back the way they had come.

The Arab knew now that any further prevarication was useless and he sullenly agreed to show Saad the way. First they called at a near-by Army post to find reinforcements, quickly provided on production of Ashton's letter. Then the Arab began to give directions. Before long the track became so rough that even the Jeeps could not make it, and the whole party had to disembark and start walking. The further they went the harder was the going. They were actually moving along the Wady Ta'amireh which runs from the south-east of Bethlehem to the Dead Sea, disgorging finally through the Wady Darajeh or Murabba'at (see map on p. 8).

For seven hours the party stumbled on. Many times Saad looked at their guide, wondering if he were not deliberately misleading them, and as often he reminded the Arab that he and his military escort would not find it amusing if this were so. But the man merely shrugged his shoulders and carried on, and the party followed.

Now and again Saad caught sight of a lone figure amongst the crags about them. He knew then that their arrival would not go unheralded, but at least it seemed they were approaching something worth guarding. Gradually the wady in which they were walking became a great gorge with sides hundreds of feet high. Then, suddenly, rounding a bend, they saw the tell-tale clouds of dust rising from two great cave entrances high up in the almost vertical cliff face. As they watched, rocks tumbled out of the gaping holes and crashed into the wady bed. They had arrived.

Someone began shouting from the top of the cliffs, and a dozen or so Bedouin emerged from the caves and started climbing into the surrounding crags. Saad's party hurried on, dividing into groups to try and head off and capture the clandestine excavators. The soldiers fired a round or two in the air and called on the Bedouin to surrender. Meanwhile Saad and his bodyguard climbed up to the nearest cave.

They found themselves in a great vaulted chamber, the very size of which made them stare in amazement. It stretched back some fifty yards into the hillside, its roof twelve to fifteen feet high and in places over twenty feet wide. The dust of the illicit excavations still hung heavily in the air and one glance was enough to tell them that the floor of the cave had been thoroughly worked over. Only a fully equipped archaeological team could hope now to do more than the Bedouin.

The soldiers had by now rounded up as many of the excavators as they could find and searched them without success. When questioned, they confessed that magnificent finds had been made here, but, of course, always by other people. They pressed Saad and his escort to remain there the night, but although every muscle in his body craved for sleep, Joseph refused. He knew that the chances of keeping their unwilling guide with them until the morning were negligible, and he was still their one link between the caves and the documents. So wearily the party started back the way they had come, with another seven hours' walk before them. Eventually they reached the place where they had left their transport, bade farewell to their commandeered reserves, and drove on to deposit their hostage with the Bethlehem constabulary.

It was morning by the time Saad and his friend reached Jerusalem. Joseph contacted the local Inspector of Antiquities and reported on the search, sending along the piece of sandal and scroll fragment. Then he dropped exhausted on to his bed and slept.

He awoke later in the day to find the city in an uproar. His 'kidnapping' and incarceration of the Arab had been noised abroad by the man's friends in Bethlehem, and the civilian authorities were demanding to know why the Army should have so treated a respectable citizen of the kingdom. It took some time for the furore to calm down and Saad was never allowed to forget the incident.

In the meantime, the local Inspector of Antiquities, Dr Awni Dajani (now Director), with one of Saad's companions to guide him, made his way to the Murabba'at caves and took with him a party from the American School. They reported on their return to Harding and De Vaux, confirming Saad's account of the size and present state of the caves, but nothing was done.

Looking back, it was perhaps a mistake to have used force to elicit information from the Bedouin. Something similar was done in 1961, but then it merely succeeded in driving precious documents even farther underground, making them even harder to recover and perhaps even endangering their further preservation. All the same, having obtained the required information at such a cost of physical effort and good will, it is difficult to understand why the discovery was not immediately exploited and full archaeological excavations put in hand.

One reason may have been that at this time Scrolls discoveries in the Dead Sea area were beginning to come so quickly that resources, archaeological and financial, in Jordan were insufficient to cope with the demands. Why then, one may reasonably ask, were not the doors flung open to all comers, suitably financed and archaeologically trained and equipped to try to take the initiative from the Bedouin? Whatever the reason, a singular lack of resourcefulness was then displayed by all concerned. No general invitation was issued, no major public fund for the recovery of these priceless documents was then organized, and the 'official' excavation of the Murabba'at caves was not arranged for another three months.

Then, in January 1952, four caves were thoroughly explored; and the material that has come from them (mostly by purchase from the Bedouin) must be reckoned as some of the most amazing archaeological treasure that has ever come out of Palestine. It ranges from a wooden adze handle, complete with leather thongs for binding on the flint blade and dateable to 4000–3000 B.C. (pl. 7a), to letters written by the leader of the Second Jewish Revolt in the second century of our era. These finds are probably quite unconnected with the cache of documents found by the shepherd lad, but are exciting enough (see Appendix II).

Some of the clandestine diggers were employed by the

official party at Murabba'at; but, whilst they were earning their honest bread, their brethren were continuing the great scroll hunt with added zeal. Eleven miles to the north, they were busy again in the vicinity of the 1947 cave, and even while Harding and De Vaux worked at the Murabba'at caves, news came through of another find in the original area. Harding immediately went there on his own, and, not far from the site of the first cave, saw a cloud of dust from high up in the cliffs which betokened the activities of the Ta'amireh archaeologists. There was nothing he could do on his own, so, turning his car, he drove as quickly as possible to Jericho and begged the services of two soldiers of the Arab Legion. With these he was able to round up four of the diggers, but the rest melted away, taking with them any fragments they may have had. These were later bought through the usual channels, but in the meantime it was decided, somewhat belatedly, to organize an expedition to cover the whole of the original area, searching for more caves and fully excavating the one recently found. The French and American Schools combined their resources for this work and covered an area of some five miles along the cliffs, exploring over two hundred caves or clefts in the rock. The clearing of the Second Cave produced very little more inscribed material and, apart from the famous 'copper scroll' from the Third Cave (pl. 14, 15; Appendix III), which was found together with some parchment fragments, no more written documents were discovered by this expedition, which is described in more detail in the next chapter. With the purchase of the Murabba'at cache and the fragments from the Second Cave, the resources of the Museum and the French School were pretty well exhausted; indeed, Harding had borrowed several thousand pounds from the bank on behalf of the Museum in order to buy what he had, trusting that when the full realization of what was happening became known to the world, money would soon flow in to replace it.

It was thus with some apprehension, as well as excitement, that some months later, on 18 September 1952, Harding received a telephone call from Father De Vaux in Jerusalem saying that he had been offered an enormous quantity of fragments from a new source, and that after long negotiation he had purchased one lot for thirteen hundred pounds. The new cave was again in the area of the original discovery, and Harding collected two soldiers and went straight down to the Dead Sea once more.

Sure enough, there was the cloud of dust, but this time not in the cliffs. It arose from the edge of the marly plateau that extends like a shelf from the foot of the cliffs towards the coastal plain (pl. 4a). What was most galling was the fact that Harding had himself, with other archaeologists, been working only a stone's throw away from the new cave a few months previously. They had been excavating some ruins at a site known as Khirbet ('ruins of') Qumran (the first letter is pronounced with a hard *k* from the back of the throat; locally it is often given a *g* sound), named after the wady, or seasonal river bed, that runs by its southern end from the cliffs to the Sea. These ruins (pl. 16a) turned out to be the home of the sect owning the scrolls library (see Chapter 5), but for some reason the search of the area for more scroll caves had missed out the immediate vicinity of the ruined settlement. This oversight, like another not far to the north, was to cost us dearly over the next few years.

The Bedouin scroll-hunters had made their discovery near the ruins as the result of a tip passed on to them by one of the elders of the tribe. It appears that he had been dozing over the camp fire one evening, only half-listening to the excited prattle of the younger men as they discussed the recent excavations at Qumran. Suddenly something one of them said struck a chord in his memory. Many years before, whilst he was yet a young man, he had been out shooting partridge in this area. One of the birds had fallen wounded behind him on the plateau and flapped its way along the edge of a precipice to disappear through a narrow crevice in the marl. The hunter had followed it with some difficulty and had found himself in a large chamber, hewn out of the terrace (pl. 4b). In a niche in the wall he had found a small pottery lamp which he knew to be ancient, and on the floor several pieces of broken jars. He had wondered at these strange finds, but rescued his quarry and then forgot the incident until reminded of it by the camp-fire talk.

The next day the young men set off to rediscover the Cave of the Wounded Partridge, taking with them their bare necessities, a bag of meal, a little water, ropes, and a primitive oil lamp. After a while they found the cave, and let one of their number down on ropes to effect an entrance in the precipitous edge of the plateau. His courage was well rewarded. After burrowing through several feet of thick choking dust on the chamber floor his groping hands came on a compact layer of tens of thousands of scroll fragments. These he and his friends excavated as fast as they could, knowing the time at their disposal before officialdom should hear of the discovery was limited. They worked in shifts through several days, and it was the morning shift that Harding disturbed. Little remained then for the archaeologists to find and most of the cache – the remains, as we later found, of several hundred documents – had to be bought back from the illicit excavators as and when money became available.

This cave was numbered Four, and investigation in the immediate vicinity brought to light another similar artificially hollowed chamber containing a few badly weathered pieces, and numbered Five. This search also identified another cave at the foot of the cliffs, the contents of which had previously been bought by the Museum, and this was known as Cave Six.

A serious financial situation had now arisen. The price of scroll fragments was still standing at a pound per square centimetre, and although with all this new material it might be expected to drop somewhat, it was clear that tens of thousands of pounds were going to be required to save this fabulous library. Kando was now acting as agent for the Bedouin, who were themselves well aware what the fragments were worth, and demanded from him nearly as much as he could expect to receive. Gone were the days when he could make a thousand pounds for no more trouble than a brief expedition to a cave. The Ta'amireh jealously guarded their secrets now, and their cave-hunting had become a thoroughgoing business, directed by the leaders of the tribe, and engaged in by all the able-bodied members. Nobody in the world knows that desolate area like these people, and it is certain that if it had not been for them the Dead Sea scrolls would still have remained undiscovered. If the prices are high, the work is tedious and back-breaking in the extreme, and certainly no member of a scrolls expedition who has scaled the cliffs and combed hundreds of caves, sifting the dust between his finger-tips for days on end, in a stifling atmosphere which is just indescribable, would begrudge the Ta'amireh a penny of their gains. Furthermore, as more and more material became available, and the first close examinations were made, it became increasingly evident that these scrolls were fantastically important, beyond every scholar's wildest dreams. Already, study of the 1947 scrolls was producing any number of parallels with the New Testament, and these and the material from this and the later caves were clearly going to change every textbook on this period of Judaism and Christian origins that had ever been written. Even the tiniest fragment was of value, since the chances were that it could be joined to others, perhaps in a vital spot, throwing new light on the messianic expectations of the times, or the theological conceptions current among the Sect owning the scrolls, of whom till now we had seemed to know practically nothing.

Harding, then, rightly felt it his duty to save as much of the material as possible at all costs. From all sides letters came pouring in saying how valuable and exciting these finds were going to be. The newspapers carried long articles drawing the public attention to the miraculous finds by the Dead Sea. Harding himself could say publicly that this was the biggest archaeological discovery ever made in Palestine, and, taking into consideration this vital period in man's history, there seemed good grounds for saying the most important anywhere at any time. In short, the world of scholarship was brought to a fever-pitch of interest and excitement, and articles poured into the learned presses all over the world. The only commodity which did not appear was money.

Harding appealed to his Government. Jordan's budget is ridiculously small when compared with that of Britain, France, or the United States. Every penny has to be put to urgent use, and development schemes cry out for attention if the meagre resources of the country are to be stretched to support an abnormally swollen population. With an enemy at her gates, she must for ever keep a standing army at the alert, which, even with outside help, drains her reserves intolerably. Yet, when confronted with the situation by their Director of Antiquities, who pointed out the value of these scrolls, particularly for Christian scholarship, this Muslim community found fifteen thousand pounds from its slender purse to buy scroll fragments. Let it be realized that this was not the careless gesture of some millionaire seeking social prestige among his countrymen. The money came out of the public funds, and urgent agricultural and health schemes were delayed because of it.

But it was soon spent, and still fragments poured in from the Ta'amireh. Harding could expect no more financial aid from the Government. People abroad, perhaps unaware of the desperate situation, were showing no practical interest in rescuing the fragments, though full of wonder and fulsome praise when they were saved. True the price had now gone down to ten shillings per square centimetre, but thousands more were urgently needed. Harding decided to go again to his Government with what must have been an even harder request. If he could induce foreign bodies to buy these fragments, would the Government lift its very strict law against the export of antiquities and let the fragments leave the country once their message had been correlated with other pieces, joined wherever possible to their original documents, and published? Obviously this work had to be done in one place, since once the pieces were distributed they could never be put together. But it would mean that these precious documents would leave their own country and, like too many of the treasures of the ancient East, be sent all over the globe to be the pride and joy of foreign museums. It would have been natural enough for the Jordan Government to have refused this request. After all, there was always the hope that eventually some institution would give the money regardless of what they themselves would get out of it – considering the saving of this priceless material for mankind reward enough in itself. But, perhaps regrettably, the Government did not refuse. Harding was able to send a circular to all the great academic institutions of the world offering to 'sell' these fragments to them, providing the money was immediately forthcoming and that it was understood that delivery could not be expected until they had been completely edited and published as a whole. The first response came from the McGill University of Canada. A widowed lady subscribed fifteen thousand dollars for the purchase of the fragments in memory of her husband. Then the Vatican in Rome gave about seven hundred pounds and, later, several thousand. A friend of Manchester University subscribed a thousand pounds, and the University itself doubled this amount. In the spring of 1955, Professor K. G. Kuhn brought to Jordan about £4,500, for the purchase of fragments. It was a fund raised jointly between the Federal Government at Bonn and the Government of Baden-Württemberg on behalf of the University of Heidelberg.

The German money brought forth some very large pieces, and we firmly believed that these were the long hoarded 'reserves' now coming to light, thus heralding the end of the struggle to retrieve the contents of this fabulous cave. But in the summer of 1956, privately subscribed funds received via the McCormick Theological Seminary of Chicago, and the remainder of the Vatican money, brought in still more Fourth Cave material. But this, we were assured by Kando, really was the end. And so we believed until, in the summer of 1958, five thousand more dollars from a Unitarian community in Manhattan attracted into the fold several more sizeable pieces, including a large fragment of Deuteronomy dating perhaps to the third pre-Christian century. Kando swears that this is the last of that cave's manuscript treasures: we are sceptical.

In any case, other finds have been made which have only complicated the situation. Although the small caches numbered seven to ten were found by the archaeologists, close by the ruins of the monastery, the third, perhaps even the second, greatest discovery since Cave One fell to the Bedouin in January 1956. And it came at a very awkward moment. The political events culminating in the Suez affair resulted in the dismissal of Harding not long after the discovery. Relations between the Palestine Archaeological Museum and the Jordan Government worsened considerably, with the faults by no means all on one side.

Cave Eleven, as it is now called, is situated between One and Three, fairly low in the cliffs to the north of Qumran and easily accessible. Looking at the cave now, it is difficult to understand how it could have been missed by the archaeologists during their 1952 search of the cliffs. In fact it was almost certainly searched then or previously; but the probes, for want of either sufficient lighting equipment or determination, had not gone far enough. It appears that a roof-fall at the back of the cave had been mistaken for solid rock. Further investigation by Bedouin in 1956 beyond the fall revealed a small recess in which had been neatly piled a hoard of manuscripts. Just how many were found then we still do not know, since only part of the cache came immediately into Museum hands. The remainder, including at least two more scrolls, glimpsed in Arab hands by two scholars without opportunity for further investigation, have apparently disappeared from the face of the earth.

The scroll and fragments that were taken into custody by the Museum were locked in a safe and nobody allowed to study their contents or even photograph them fully. Eighteen months later the purchase price of forty-eight thousand pounds was paid over quietly to Kando by the Museum authorities, who were obliged to liquidate a large part of the Museum trust funds in order to do so. Very little information about the discovery was made public, and still no general appeal for funds was launched.

Four or five years after the find, the documents began to make their reappearance from the confines of the Museum, and in most extraordinary circumstances. The trustees – only one of whom, Father Roland De Vaux, O.P., can claim any competence in reading or appreciating the significance of these most important and controversial documents – apparently began offering the publication and exhibition rights to the highest bidders. Thus, for instance, in 1962 a Divinity School in the United States was persuaded to pay some twenty-five thousand pounds for the right to publish the prize of the Cave Eleven collection in Museum hands, an unrolled scroll of the Biblical Psalms. Enough had been seen, from a leaf broken away from the scroll, to identify the work generally, although the order of the Psalms was seen to be at variance with the standard texts, and the wording slightly different. Subsequent investigation showed that the collection included a number of psalms not included in the Hebrew version hitherto known.

The Dutch Government was offered the right to publish a badly damaged scroll of an Aramaic translation of Job, most interesting since it was known to have been suppressed by the Jewish authorities some years after this copy was deposited in the Qumran cave.

A less fortunate transaction was similarly invited for a 'scroll' of Ezekiel. This was known to be in a bad condition, but nevertheless one American institution offered some three thousand pounds for the privilege of opening and publishing it (negotiations are said to have started at around seven thousand pounds!). A scholar of high repute was sent to Jordan to edit the scroll; and an expert in the preservation of antiquities, formerly of the British Museum, was called from Rome to undertake the delicate task of unrolling the document. The ransom handed over, the 'scroll' was then produced. The hearts of the recipients must have sunk when they first saw their prize. As anyone with any experience of working with these two-thousand-year-old pieces of parchment could have told them instantly, their journeys had been largely in vain. At some stage in the life of the scroll, water must have poured through it, reducing the parchment to almost solid glue. The preservations expert did manage to peel a few more fragments from the outside, but then abandoned hope and took a saw to the remainder, leaving a couple of pieces of glue on which no writing was legible. The scroll, indeed, could never have been unrolled, its convolutions had become for the most part merged together and its stratified structure lost by gelatinization. The trustees did at least refund most of the purchase price.

Meanwhile, the work on the Cave Four material having been nearly completed as far as the initial editing was concerned, the Jordan Government began to have wise second thoughts on the desirability of dispersing the fragments around the world. They asked the 1952 donors to accept the return of their money rather than the pieces. Although in some quarters this brought forth howls of protest, it was of course a wise decision. Otherwise scholars wishing to check our readings or joins of the fragments might have to travel to any of half a dozen countries to track them down. The chances of joining a hitherto unidentified fragment with its companion pieces, lodged perhaps thousands of miles away, would be negligible.

But the problem of the recovery of the clandestinely excavated documents and their adequate protection and availability for prompt publication still remains. One would like to see established in Jordan an institute, free from sectarian, religious, or political control, where the scrolls might be kept for all time, available to scholars from all lands for study and research. Here students could be trained in the arts of palaeography, archaeology, and Near Eastern culture generally, forming a body of trained reserves capable of dealing immediately with any future finds. Here, too, Arab and Western students could meet on common ground, and in their common studies and research further the cause of mutual tolerance and understanding that is the scrolls' greatest promise to mankind.

A start towards this ideal has been made. In 1961, the present writer with a few friends took the initiative and organized a public charity called the Dead Sea Scrolls Fund with these declared aims. Already generous donations in money and equipment have enabled us to make several small winter expeditions into the Wilderness of Judaea to search for more scroll caves on a systematic plan. In Jordan we have found enthusiastic support from His Majesty King Hussein, his government, and armed services, so that the way has been opened up into this vast treasure-house of the desert as never before. All now depends on whether this freely offered help in Jordan can be matched with financial and moral support from other countries.

CHAPTER THREE

THE EDITING OF THE SCROLLS
AND FRAGMENTS

SEVEN documents were taken from the First Cave at Qumran: two manuscripts of the Book of Isaiah, a manual of creed and conduct of the Jewish sect owning the scrolls, a collection of thanksgiving psalms, an order of battle for an apocalyptic war between the Children of Light and the Children of Darkness, a commentary on the Book of Habakkuk, and another scroll which appears to be a pseud-epigraphic elaboration of the book of Genesis, written in Aramaic. The Hebrew University had one of the Isaiah scrolls, the hymns, and the war scroll in its possession and released extracts from them in two successive editions of a small work. Seven years after they had come into Sukenik's hands they were published in full with an introduction in Hebrew, and later with the introduction translated into English. In the meantime, the Americans had published the other Isaiah scroll, the Habakkuk commentary, and the *Manual of Discipline*, as the sectarian work was called, within three years of their arriving in the country in the hands of the Syrian Metropolitan. Unfortunately, before they could get the Aramaic scroll opened – it was in a very poor state of preservation – the time-limit set by the Metropolitan ran out and he refused to let them continue on the work. He seems to have been hoping that the one unpublished work among the collection would keep the price high, although it was not until 1955 that he managed to sell the complete set to a private purchaser, who bought it on behalf of the Israeli Government, despite the questionable ownership of the property, for something like a quarter of a million dollars.

The editing and publication of a complete scroll is a

relatively simple task. The reading here and there may be difficult, but at least where the scroll is intact the position of the words and phrases is not in doubt. Very different is the preparation of hundreds of tiny fragments, many no bigger than a fingernail (pl. 10b). All these must be laid out and minutely examined in the hope that they may connect with parent documents and be of use in reconstructing broken passages. The work of editing the fragments bought and excavated from the First Cave was entrusted to Fathers J. T. Milik and D. Barthélemy, both attached to the French School in Jerusalem. Starting work in 1952, the edition appeared in 1955, having taken two full years to go through the press. It is not surprising that the second-named collaborator was soon after flown home for extended medical treatment, although Milik has been able to continue on the work of preparing the Semitic texts of Murabba'at and, at the same time, by far the largest section of the fragments from the Fourth Cave.

As the Cave Four material flowed in, it became clear that its bulk was going to surpass by far anything found in the First Cave, and that it was beyond the capabilities of one or two scholars to edit in a reasonable time. Lankester Harding therefore decided that the work should be shared by a team of scholars brought to Jerusalem and resident there for this purpose over several years, or at least for one year with return visits of several months each. Since the excavations have always been carried out by joint teams drawn from the French and American Schools, with the co-directorship of Lankester Harding, an Englishman, it was further decided that the Scrolls team should be of an international character. Thus there have been drawn to Jerusalem for this exciting work men from America, Britain, France, Germany, and Poland – eight of us in all. The division of work has been roughly that the two American scholars, Dr Frank Cross and Father Patrick Skehan, have taken the biblical section, the remains, in all, of about a hundred different manuscripts, Father Jean Starcky the Aramaic works, Dr Claus Hunzinger the copies of the war scroll and some papyrus manuscripts, Father Milik the apocryphal and pseudepigraphical works, the Manual and Damascus Document manuscripts, and other sectarian works, Mr John Strugnell the hymn scrolls and other non-biblical works, and myself the Bible commentaries and some wisdom literature (pl. 11a). The material from the other caves has been put in the care of Father Maurice Baillet of France. Even when we are not able to be in Jerusalem, much can be done on the photographs which we take to our home countries with us, but reference to the original pieces has been absolutely essential to the work.

The fragments reach the Museum from Kando or the Bedouin in cigarette cartons and the like, and are immediately cleaned of the white dust with which most are covered. Sometimes this is so firmly engrained that no amount of brushing will remove it, and then we find that a very light brushing with a camel hair brush touched with a non-acid oil, like castor oil, will make the marl translucent and bring up the writing very clearly. Very often it is not so much the dust that obliterates the writing as the colour of the leather itself, which has gone completely black from exposure to humidity and thus makes the writing indistinguishable from its surroundings. In these cases the process of infra-red photography has been particularly valuable in our work. The results on fragments where to the naked eye no writing at all was visible are just amazing, and to this miracle we owe a very great deal of relief from serious eye-strain.

Very often the skin of the fragment is dry and brittle, sometimes tightly curled, and then it must undergo a process of hydration before it is safe to unroll it. The pieces requiring treatment are put into a glass vessel containing water at the bottom covered with a zinc perforated sheet and a sealed lid. After ten or fifteen minutes in hot weather the fragment is usually supple enough to allow gentle manipulation, but sometimes, with particularly coarse pieces, several hours of such treatment is necessary. If the piece is left too long, the result is a drop of liquid glue and one less epoch-making discovery. The clean fragments are laid out between the glass plates, several dozen or scores in each, and put out in the large room on trestle tables (pl. 10a).

To the new collaborator entering the Museum 'Scrollery' for the first time, the effect was rather shattering. He found himself surrounded by about five hundred glass plates, packed with fragments of varying sizes, over which he would be spending the next year or two of his life crouching, trying to pick out pieces belonging to his documents, or seeking to identify new fragments. If he was a comparatively late-comer to the team, perhaps some of the results already obtained would strengthen his weakening resolve. In the corners of the room were the collected sections of other members of the team, and walking round he could see how pieces, no larger than the palm of a hand, had grown to cover complete columns of text, and whose secrets would be proudly shown to him by the collaborator responsible. He might look wonderingly at a biblical text which is going to bring about a revolution in our ideas of text transmission, or on a commentary which throws new light on the messianic expectations of the time. He might find himself gazing at the Aramaic text of pseudepigraphical work never before seen in its original tongue, and all around him were biblical texts older by a thousand years, and more, than Hebrew manuscripts of the Bible previously known. He would have walked into a new and exciting world, but the way to the revealing of its treasures was a hard one, and before he could be sitting down reading columns of text and preparing the transcriptions and translations for publication, he had many months of extremely trying work ahead of him. Armed with one of his biggest fragments he would go slowly round those scores of unidentified plates seeking for the lost pieces. As he grew more proficient at the task he would be able to recognize a member of his flock from one letter or even part of a letter. One of the saving factors has been that of the four hundred or so manuscripts we have had to deal with, surprisingly few were written by the same scribe, so that by recognizing the idiosyncrasies of one's own scribes one could be fairly sure that the piece belonged to his document. Of course, this was not always so, and often we would find, after some months of patient collecting, that we had more than one work on a plate, coming from the hand of the same scribe. However, besides the script there was the rather less dependable criterion for identification of the skin itself. Where this remains constant over the whole scroll, it could be a most useful means of quickly recognizing parts from the same work. But, unfortunately, there are often extreme variations in colour and even texture where different skins have been sewn together to complete the work, or where disintegration of the scroll in antiquity has meant that different conditions have acted upon the pieces. Thus one fragment might be clean and supple, while its neighbour is darkened with moisture and warped completely out of shape. Warping is a major problem, for not only does it make pieces very difficult to join together even where the join is certain from the text, but it will distort the letters of the writing out of the true form, so that if there are only one or two letters on the piece, and the colour of the leather is changed from its parent document, it may be a long time before it is recognized as belonging to its own scroll.

Another cause of difficulty in joining is that worms or damp have often attacked the edges of fragments, so that real 'jig-saw puzzle' joins are no longer possible. This again is largely due to the scrolls' having disintegrated in antiquity, and so frequently does this occur, and so often does one find tears which are certainly not new (pl. 13a), that I am myself inclined to believe that the Fourth Cave documents at least were torn up in antiquity, perhaps before being placed in the chamber (pl. 13b). Be that as it may, much of the relative positioning of the fragments in a document has to be done by 'dead reckoning' rather than edge-to-edge joins. This is not too difficult in the case of a biblical text where the order of the words is already known, although sources of trouble here are variant texts which we shall discuss in the next chapter. It is more difficult in the case of non-biblical works previously quite unknown or known only in translation.

An intriguing problem which has presented itself during the work has been the deciphering of a number of different secret codes in which several of the works were written. Happily they are nothing more complicated than new alphabets, which were composed by the Sectarians to keep certain works especially secret, and in one case they contrive to write most, but not all, of the words backwards, and use a mixture of four or five alphabets, including one or two of their own invention. Thus, for instance, one might come across a word written with a combination of alphabets in something after this fashion: ΧꙀγ'Ϧ ϜΥ ⊼ΥΟρ ⊙⊼Χ. The reader might like to work that one out for himself, with the clue that the alphabets represented in this imaginary English phrase are Latin, Greek, Phoenician, and Aramaic, and the principle of using ancient letters for their modern equivalents is precisely that used by the author of this Qumran document. Having deciphered one column including a particularly puzzling phrase, it was encouraging to find another piece in a further purchase which contained the same phrase written, rather carelessly for the coder, in 'clear' Hebrew, confirming the decipherment.

Another code used entirely letters of their own invention, and begins in 'clear' Hebrew: 'the wisdom which he spoke to the Sons of the Dawn,' and then goes on into this unknown script, beginning 'Listen ye.' One day, when the three of us, who then constituted the team, were tired of cleaning the thousands of fragments in the boxes before us, we decided to enliven the proceedings by having a competition to see who could crack the code first. The main difficulty was that being very fragmentary there were very few complete words, so that determining the relative frequency of occurrence of letters, which would normally have given the answer in a very short time, would not work so easily in this instance. Some of the letters looked something like the proto-Hebraic writing, a derivation from the ancient Phoenician script, but they made no sense when given these equivalents. Whilst Cross and I were tearing our hair over it after lunch that day, Milik strolled in and informed us that he had done it, or at least got enough of the letters to make a full decipherment eventually possible. He had guessed the meaning of one of the few complete words, which had the pattern *ABCBAD*. Since Hebrew is based on the triliteral root system there are not a large number of words possible with this combination, and a common group *LHTHLK*, the infinitive of the reflexive form of the verb *HLK* with the prefix *L*, meaning 'to walk about', gave him enough letters to break other smaller words, and thence to work through the whole fragment until he had the alphabet, or as much of it as could be obtained from the evidence available. There are, however, other cryptic scripts which have been impossible to decipher so far for want of sufficient material.

I have said that a factor which is apt to give trouble is the changing of skins part-way through a scroll. Just as at times like this one wishes there had existed animals with skins large enough to suffice for a complete scroll, we often wish they had invented the fountain pen in the first century B.C. Some of our scribes seem to have had 'quill trouble', in that the instrument kept wearing down and giving the writing a quite different appearance from that presented when the scribe had newly sharpened his pen. I have one manuscript in my section, a commentary on Isaiah, in which the writing changes startlingly in the first two columns, and fragments coming from later columns look different again. Of course, close examination shows the same basic characteristics are still there, but when one is looking through fragments of only one or two letters for pieces to match, these variations can be most puzzling. It is by no means unknown, also, for the Qumran Scriptorium to play a very mean trick on the Jerusalem Scrollery by changing horses in midstream, or rather scribes in mid-scroll. This is quite unforgivable, and most trying.

CHAPTER FOUR

THE BIBLICAL TEXTS

"THERE is, indeed, no probability that we shall ever find manuscripts of the Hebrew text going back to a period before the formation of the text which we know as Massoretic. "

Thus wrote a very great textual scholar in 1939. Happily Sir Frederick Kenyon lived to see the wonderful disproving of his words in 1948, and would no doubt have been among the first to acclaim the later Qumran discoveries in the biblical field had he only been spared a little longer. For the fact is that with these finds from Qumran we have penetrated the Massoretic barrier by more than two hundred years, and produced texts from quite distinct traditions dating from as early as the third century B.C. To grasp some idea of what this means for the future of Old Testament text criticism, we should, perhaps, recount some of the basic facts about the transmission and versions of our Bible.

Our standard translations of the Old Testament are based on relatively late manuscripts going back no further than the ninth or tenth centuries of our era. As the very latest book of our Protestant Canon was written in the second century B.C., this considerable gap might seem to throw doubt on the reliability of our text were it not for the extraordinary care with which the Jewish scribes have transmitted their sacred writings. The most exacting rules were laid down in Talmudic works for the procedure to be followed in copying the Scriptures, and such was the accuracy with which this work was done in the synagogue rolls, that all the evidence available seems to point to a fairly consistent text tradition which goes back to the first century A.D. There was a very good reason for this. When in A.D. 70 the centre of Jewish life and culture was destroyed with the fall of Jerusalem, the religious observances of the

Dispersion centred more and more on the Law, the first five
books of the Bible; and its study took the place of the Temple
as the centre of Judaism. It was therefore essential for the
unity of the Faith that the text of this work should be
standardized and given the authority of the one favoured
recension, from which no serious variants would be allowed.
A synod was convened at Jamnia, near Jaffa, between
A.D. 90 and 100, at which certain disputed questions regarding the acceptability of some of the books were decided.
At this time also, besides the extent of the Canon, the type of
text to be used as standard must have been agreed upon,
and perhaps even the type of script in which future copies
of the Law would be written. Later, the ruling of the page,
the size of columns, gaps between words and sentences, and
even the colour and nature of the ink to be used and the
clothing worn by the scribe were determined for all time.
Thus, from the end of the first century, the standard text
of the Bible was more or less fixed and has been preserved
for us to the present time with remarkably few variations.
But it is important to realize that the Jamnia Synod did not
compose a standard text, or even make an eclectic version
from many traditions, but settled on one particular textual
tradition as the norm for all time. They selected one
from a number circulating in Jewish circles prior to that
time, and it is in this matter of variant traditions of the pre-
Jamnia period that the Qumran evidence is particularly
valuable.

The new standard text, which, with all its deficiencies as
well as excellences, has been brought down to us and which
lies behind our English translations, is called *Massoretic*.
Actually to apply this term to it in its earlier stages is an
anachronism, for the very important work of the Massoretes,
the body of Jewish scholars who systematized the *Massorah*,
or 'tradition', did not begin until the seventh century. At
that time these scholars set themselves to sort out the mass
of traditional material which had grown up over questions
of the true pronunciation and thus interpretation of the
sacred text over the preceding centuries. In the Semitic

languages in their early written forms, this question of traditional pronunciation is particularly important, for the text is furnished with practically no vowel signs, the nearest equivalent being the use of *w* and *y*, which approximate to the vowels *u* and *i*, and are thus used to denote those sounds. On the whole this defective system works quite well in literature with which the reader is well acquainted, and it is indeed surprising to the European student of the Semitic languages to discover how easily vowel signs can be dispensed with in reading. The real difficulties begin when the language ceases to be a living tongue and the consonantal text becomes sacred to the point where every word is regarded as of supreme importance for matters of faith and conduct. Of course, the forces of oral tradition as well as the natural sense of the context are usually sufficient to carry the reader along, but the size of the written body of tradition which had been accumulated over certain difficult readings was ample evidence that something more permanent and definitive was required to ensure uniformity of faith and practice among the Dispersion. Hence the work of the Massoretes, who, in imitation of the Syriac vowel system, invented sets of symbols for Hebrew and thus to a great degree 'fixed' the text of the Bible even more completely than Jamnia. But it must be appreciated that this 'fixing' was an essentially artificial process, since there still existed many different ways of reading certain words or phrases, and the selection of one in each case by the Massoretes, with an occasional recognition of another, was to some extent subjective, and the traditions they rejected often went back to a very early period, as we know from early translations and now from the Qumran documents. However, when we speak of the *Massoretic Text* (MT) it will be understood that we are referring to this first-century tradition, embroidered with vowels and critical apparatus by the Massoretes of the seventh century, which forms the basis of our present editions of the Hebrew Bible and its translations.

The aim of modern biblical textual criticism is to establish, as far as possible, the original reading of the Scriptures, using all the means in our possession. These include, besides the standard Hebrew text with its Massorah, ancient translations which sometimes go back to the time before Christ, and certainly the most important of these is the Greek version. It is extant in manuscripts which go back to the very early Christian times and which contain works which, after a considerable period of uncertainty, were eventually excluded from our Hebrew Canon and now form part of our English Apocrypha. The history of this translation traditionally goes back to the third century B.C. when, under Ptolemy Philadelphus of Egypt (285–246 B.C.), a number of Jewish scholars were brought to Alexandria to make a Greek recension of the Jewish Scriptures. The story runs that the king was urged to do this by his librarian, who had heard of the wonder of these books, and he accordingly sent an envoy laden with fabulous gifts to the High Priest in Jerusalem. His request made and granted, six scholars from each of the twelve tribes of Israel were selected, and the seventy-two worthies were dispatched to Alexandria to begin their work, carrying with them a copy of the Law written in letters of gold. After a wonderful reception, they set about their task, working separately at first, but later comparing results, and finally producing the Greek translation which henceforth became known as the Septuagint (LXX), or version of the 'Seventy'. The story later gained more fantastic accretions, and tells how the translators were shut up in cells, or by pairs in thirty-six cells, and produced versions in exactly seventy-two days, which, when subjected to mutual comparison, were found to be in exact agreement with one another, thus proving that the work was the inspiration of God. The general tradition does seem to have the kernel of truth that the work was done first in Alexandria about this time, and that the Law was the first to be translated. The other books of the Old Testament were added later by different translators who varied enormously in competence and style, so that the general standard is uneven.

The LXX became at once the Bible of Greek-speaking Jews and had a wide distribution throughout the Mediterranean world. With the rise of Gentile Christianity, it became the Bible of the early Church, and since it began to be used by Christian theologians in theological disputes with the Jews, it soon lost favour with the latter, who began to prepare rival Greek versions. The most important of these was that of Aquila, made in the middle of the second century A.D., a most literal rendering which appears to be based on a Hebrew text more in accordance with that of the Massoretic Text than that underlying LXX. This was keenly used by the Jews for debate and instruction, and its use was not scorned by scholarly Christians like Origen and Jerome. Half a century later appeared the version of Theodotion. His Hebrew text was nearer to Aquila's and ours than LXX's, but how far he relied upon the early translation is disputed, and it may be that recent finds in the Dead Sea area will serve to clarify the issue (see Appendix II). Theodotion's work had a great effect on the transmission of the LXX, particularly as regards the books of Daniel and Job, and perhaps others. On the other hand, it does look as if his peculiar Daniel text did not originate with him but was already to hand at his time, as would seem to be indicated by the new evidence referred to above. A fourth version was prepared by Symmachus, writing a short time after Theodotion. His main characteristic is a much freer and consequently a better Greek style, but the remains of his work are very fragmentary and his influence on the transmission of the LXX small.

In the first half of the third century, an Alexandrian named Origen, finding in existence three other Greek versions of the Old Testament besides the LXX, which often conflicted with one another, set about making a more perfect version than them all, and produced the famous Hexapla, or six-fold version, with the first column containing the Hebrew of the current standard text, the second the Hebrew transliterated into Greek letters, the third the Greek of Aquila, the fourth of Symmachus, the fifth of the

LXX as revised by Origen himself, and the sixth the Greek of Theodotion. Origen's own revised LXX, the fifth column, later gained a currency on its own, very often less the critical apparatus appended to it by the compiler, so that in effect it became yet another version in its own right and considerably influenced the transmission of the text.

This much abridged account of the LXX's history will suffice to show that it has had a good many influences working on it to bring it to a closer uniformity with the Hebrew of the Massoretic Text, yet despite this, and this is the main point of our study, it is quite clear that at base it represents a different textual tradition from that of our standard Hebrew version which has reached us through the Synod of Jamnia and the Massoretes. One of the great questions of text critical scholarship has been: how far do the differences we find in the Greek version of LXX represent a different Hebrew original and how much the idiosyncrasies of the translators? Naturally, since we are dependent for our Hebrew text on a tradition which was standardized as early as the first century of our era, it is of more than passing interest to know what other text traditions looked like before this. Since, in many cases, in the historical books the LXX offers us a better reading than our Hebrew, we obviously want to know if these readings came from an original Hebrew text preferable at these points to our own, and if they do, then we ought clearly to give them as much authority as the one the Massoretes have bequeathed to us. There could be no question of accepting the Greek version of all the books of the Bible in preference to the MT, since a most cursory reading of other books, and in particular the poetic works, shows that they are on the whole little more than paraphrases, and not always good ones at that. The dream of scholars working in this field, then, has been to discover an ancient Hebrew text which clearly comes of the LXX family. Then, comparing this manuscript with the Greek of LXX, they could see for themselves how the ancient translators went about their business, what they added of their own accord and what they left out, how sound was their

knowledge of Hebrew and on what principles they dealt
with difficulties in the text. But to realize this dream would
mean recovering books of the Bible going back to the pre-
Jamnia days, and indeed, as far back towards the time of
the Greek translations as possible. Until 1952, this remained
a rather hopeless dream.

Excitement had run high among scholars when it
became known in 1948 that a cave near the Dead Sea had
produced pre-Massoretic texts of the Bible. Was it possible
that we were at last going to see traditions differing seriously
from the standard text, which would throw some important
light on this hazy period of variant traditions? In some
quarters the question was raised with some apprehension,
especially when news-hungry journalists began to talk
about changing the whole Bible in view of the latest discoveries, but closer examination showed that, on the whole,
the differences shown by the first Isaiah scroll were of little
account, and could often be explained on the basis of scribal
errors, or differing orthography, syntax, or grammatical
form. For example in ii. 3, 'to the mountain of the Lord'
is omitted; in vi. 3, the 'Holy' cry of the seraphim is given
but twice; in vii. 2, 'his heart' is missing, only 'the heart of
his people' being 'moved'. Scribal errors of some conse-
quence were those like the scribe's jumping from 'the vine
of Sibmah' in xvi. 8 to the same phrase in verse 9, leaving
out all the words in between. Sometimes he had added
words, with another passage in mind, as for instance in
xiv. 2 where 'and to their land' is made to precede 'to
their place', thinking, no doubt, of the previous verse, or he
adds 'and your fingers with iniquity' to 'your hands are
full of blood', in i. 15, thinking of lix. 3. Similarly, in chapters xxxvi–xxxix there are brief additions recalling the
differences shown in the parallel account in II Kings. The
main orthographic differences centred in the much freer
use of the 'vowel-consonants' mentioned above to facilitate
reading, and this characteristic is general in much of the
Qumran literature. The other Isaiah scroll showed an even
closer following of the standard text, even to points of

spelling, and there was a great deal of sighing with relief in some quarters, as well as a sense of disappointment in others. Articles then began to be written about the support Qumran offered to the Massoretic Text, and indeed these Isaiah manuscripts certainly did point once more to a pretty well unbroken tradition from the second century B.C. to the present day regarding this particular textual family. However, in 1953 came a discovery which was to put the matter in a very different light.

Whilst engaged one day in cleaning and assembling some fragile leather pieces of the book of Samuel from the Fourth Cave, Frank Cross noticed that at one place the text seemed to run completely contrary to MT. He checked again, and there was no doubt. He carried on brushing very gently until the next line came into view. Again the text showed marked variations, and the next few lines included a whole paragraph which was not represented in the standard Hebrew. His excitement mounting, Cross began to refer to the principal versions, and almost immediately saw that his text corresponded word for word with the Greek translation. The precious pieces joined to others, and time and time again he found positive correspondences with LXX against MT, until at the end of a week or so he was able to affirm that before him he had the answer to the text-critic's dream, a Hebrew text from the same family of tradition as that used by the ancient translators of the LXX. As the work continued, and more and more of the precious manuscript appeared, it was seen that sometimes it differed from both LXX and MT, and at others agreed with MT against LXX, but these cases were certainly in the minority. That scholars might have an idea of what had occurred, Cross published a portion of the new text in December of that year, and the following is an English translation of his reconstructed text, side by side with the LXX and the Revised Version for purposes of comparison. The square brackets show the extent of his reconstruction, which, although it may seem at first glance to leave rather a lot to conjecture, is in fact less subjective than may appear. The very neat script of the scroll, a characteristic bookhand of Qumran, makes the calculation of letters and spaces missing comparatively simple, and when the beginning, end, or middle of the line is extant, reconstruction of the lacunae with a fair degree of accuracy, once the general character of the text is known, is of little difficulty.

QUMRAN

I Samuel i. 22 – ii. 6
[But Hannah went not up with him;
for she sa]id unto her husband,
I will not go up until
[the child goes up when I have
weaned him (?)

that he may appear] before the Lord,
and there abide before [the Lord
for ever.
and I shall gi]ve him for a Nazarite
for ever, all the days of [his life.
And Elkanah her husband said unto
her],
Do what seemeth thee good;
tarry until [thou have weaned him;
only the Lo]rd [establish] that which
cometh out of thy mouth.
So the woman tarried [and gave her
son suck, until she weaned hi]m.

And she took him up to Shiloh when
[... with a calf of] three years and
bread,

[and an ephah of meal, and a bottle
of wine,

LXX

But Hannah went not up with him;
for she said unto her husband,
I will not go up until
the child goes up when I have
weaned him

and he shall appear before the Lord,
and there abide for ever.

And Elkanah her husband said unto
her,
Do what seemeth thee good;
tarry until thou have weaned him;
only the Lord establish that which
cometh out of thy mouth.
So the woman tarried and gave her
son suck, until she weaned him.

And she went up with him to Selom
with a calf of three years, and bread,

and an ephah of meal, and a bottle
of wine,

RV

But Hannah went not up;
for she said unto her husband,
I will not go up until

the child be weaned, and then I will
bring him.
that he may appear before the Lord,
and there abide for ever.

And Elkanah her husband said unto
her,
Do what seemeth thee good;
tarry until thou have weaned him;
only the Lord establish his word.

So the woman tarried and gave her
son suck until she weaned him. And
when she had weaned him.
she took him up with her, with three
bullocks,

and one ephah of meal, and a bottle
of wine,

and she entered into the house] of
the Lord in Shiloh, and the child
[with them,
And they came before the Lord;
and his father slew] the offering
as [he did year by year to the Lord;
and they (?) brought near the child;
and he sle]w [the bullock;
and Hannah, the mother of the child,
came to Eli and said,

O] my Lord, [as thy soul liveth,
I am the woman that stood by thee
here,
praying unto] the Lord.
[For this child I prayed;
and the Lord hath given me my
petition
which I asked of him:
therefore I also have granted him
to the Lo]rd: as long as
[he liveth he is granted to the Lord.
And she left] him there and she
worshipped [the Lord

and said,
My heart exulteth in the Lord],
mine horn is exalted in the Lo]rd:

and she entered into the house of
the Lord in Selom, and the child
with them
And they came before the Lord;
and his father slew the offering
which he did year by year to the Lord;
and he brought near the child, and
slew the bullock;
And Hannah, the mother of the child,
came to Eli and said,

O my lord, as thy soul liveth,
I am the woman that stood in thy
presence, by thee,
praying unto the Lord.
For this child I prayed;
and the Lord hath given me my
petition
which I asked of him:
therefore I also grant him
to the Lord: as long as
he liveth *he is* granted to the Lord.

and she said,
My heart is established in the Lord,
Mine horn is exalted in my God;

and brought him unto the house of
the Lord in Shiloh; and the child
was young,

And they slew the bullock,

and brought the child to Eli. And
she said,

O my lord, as thy soul liveth, my lord,
I am the woman that stood by thee
here,
praying unto the Lord.
For this child I prayed;
And the Lord hath given me my
petition
which I asked of him:
therefore I also have granted him
to the Lord: as long as
he liveth he is granted to the Lord.

And he worshipped the Lord there
and Hannah prayed,
and said,
My heart exulteth in the Lord,
mine horn is exalted in the Lord:

QUMRAN

my mouth is enlarged over mine
enemies;.
I rejoice in thy salvation
F[or there is none holy as the Lo[rd;
and there is none righteous as our
God;
and there is none beside] thee:
neither is there any rock like our
God.
[Talk no more proudly;
let not arrogan]cy come out of your
mouth:
for [the Lord] is a God of knowledge,
[...
The bow of the mighty me]n is
broken, and they that stumbled
are gir[ded with strength
They that were full have hired out
themselves for bread:
and the hungry ...

the barr]en hath borne seven;
and she that hath many children
languisheth.
The Lord killeth and maketh alive:
he bringeth down [to the grave,...

LXX

my mouth is enlarged over mine
enemies;
I rejoiced in thy salvation.
For there is none holy as the Lord;
and there is none righteous as our
God;
there is none holy beside thee.

Boast not, and utter not high things;
let not high-sounding words come
out of your mouth:
for the Lord is a God of knowledge,
and God prepares his own designs.
The bow of the mighty *men* has waxed
feeble, and the weak
have girded themselves with strength.
They that were full of bread are
brought low;
and the hungry have forsaken the
land;

For the barren hath borne seven;
and she that hath many children
languisheth.
The Lord killeth and maketh alive:
he bringeth down to the grave,

R V

my mouth is enlarged over mine
enemies;
because I rejoice in thy salvation.
There is none holy as the Lord;

for there is none beside thee:
neither is there any rock like our
God.
Talk no more, so exceedingly proudly;
let not arrogancy come out of your
mouth:
for the Lord is a God of knowledge,
and by him actions are weighed.
The bows of the mighty men are
broken, and they that stumbled
are girded with strength.
They that were full have hired out
themselves for bread;
and they that were hungry have
ceased;

yea, the barren hath borne seven;
and she that hath many children
languisheth.
The Lord killeth and maketh alive:
he bringeth down to the grave,

Col. II I Samuel ii. 16–25.
And the man would answer
and s[a]y to the priest's servant,
Let the priest burn the [fat] presently,
and then take for thyself
of all things which thy soul desireth:
then he would say, Nay,
but thou shalt give *it* me now;
or I shall t[ake *it*] by force.
When the flesh was seethed (?) one
would take a fleshhook of three teeth
[in his hand, and strike it] in the pot
or cauldron: [al]l that the fleshhook
brought up he would take. If [...]
good except (in the case of ?) the
'brea[st that is waved' and the?]
right [thi]gh.
And the si[n of the young men] was
very gre[at before the] Lord:
for they abhorred the offering of the
Lord.
But Samuel mini[stered before the
L]ord,
being a child, girt with a linen ephod.
[Moreover his mother] made [him a
little robe, and brou]ght it to him
from year to year, when she ca[me
up with her husband]

And *if* the man that sacrificed said,

First let the fat be burned, as it is fit,
and then take for thyself
of all things which thy soul desireth;
then he would say, Nay,
but thou shalt give *it me* now;
and if not, I will take *it* by force.

And the sin of the young men was
very great before the Lord:
for they set at nought the offering of
the Lord.
But Samuel ministered before the
Lord,
being a child, girt with a linen ephod.
Moreover his mother made him a
little robe, and brought it to him
from year to year, when she came
up with her husband

And if the man said
to him,
They will surely burn the fat presently,
and then take (for thyself)
as much as thy soul desireth;
then he would say, Nay,
but thou shalt give *it me* now;
and if not, I will take *it* by force.

And the sin of the young men was
very great before the Lord:
for men abhorred the offering of the
Lord.
But Samuel ministered before the
Lord,
being a child, girt with a linen ephod.
Moreover his mother made him a
little robe, and brought it to him
from year to year, when she came
up with her husband

QUMRAN

to offer the [yearly sacri]fice.
And Eli blessed El[kanah and his wife,]
saying,
The L[ord] recompense thee seed of this woman
fo[r the loan] which she len[t to the L]ord.
And the man went unto his own home,
And the Lo[rd] visited Hannah and she bare yet t[hr]ee sons

and two daughters.
And Sam[uel] grew before the L[ord].
Now Eli was very old;
ninety [. . .?] years of age,
and he heard what his sons did unto the children of Israel.

[And he said unto them,
Why] do ye [such things]
of which I he[ar evil] things
[from the mouth of all the people

LXX

to offer the yearly sacrifice.
And Eli blessed Elkanah and his wife
saying,
The Lord recompense thee seed of this woman
for the loan which thou hast lent to the Lord.
And the man went unto his own home,
And the Lord visited Hannah And she bare yet three sons

and two daughters.
And the child Samuel grew before the Lord.
Now Eli was very old;

And he heard what his sons did unto the children of Israel.

And he said unto them,
Why do ye according to this thing which I hear
from the mouth of all the people

R V

to offer the yearly sacrifice.
And Eli blessed Elkanah and his wife,
and said,
The Lord give thee seed of this woman
for the loan which was lent to the Lord.
And they went unto their own home.
And the Lord visited Hannah, And she conceived, and bare three sons

and two daughters.
And the child Samuel grew before the Lord.
Now Eli was very old;

and he heard all that his sons did unto all Israel, and how that they lay with the women that did service at the door of the tent of meeting.
And he said unto them,
Why do ye such things?
for I hear of your evil dealings from all this people.

of the Lord?
Nay, my sons; for it is no good re]port
that I he[ar;
do not so, for the reports] which I
hear are [not] good:
making [...

If one man should] at all sin
[against another ...]

to the Lord: but [if...

of the Lord?
Nay, *my* sons; for it is no good report
that I hear;
do not so, for the reports which I
hear are not good:
so that the people do not serve God.

If one man should at all sin
against another then shall they pray
for him
to the Lord: but if...

Nay, my sons; for it is no good report
that I hear;

ye make the Lord's people to trans-
gress.
If one man sin
against another, God shall judge him:

but if...

Two years later Dr Cross was able to publish fragments from another, older scroll of Samuel. Not only was this again shown to stand directly in the LXX tradition but it had the added interest of being probably one of the oldest manuscripts yet to be found in the Qumran library, going back, as Cross believes, to the end of the third century B.C. The LXX of the Law itself could not have been translated much before the date of this document! Briefly summarized, the results of the careful examination of these six fragments, which contain no more than about fifty complete words in all, are that, including three doubtful cases, Qumran agrees thirteen times with LXX against MT, and with MT against LXX four times. Impressive as these correspondences with LXX are for so small a selection of fragments, they do not, as Cross says, tell the whole story. The most extraordinary characteristic of this ancient witness to the text is the high proportion of original readings it preserves, which agree neither with LXX nor with MT.

Another interesting LXX-type text, this time from the Law itself, was also published by Cross's colleague on the biblical section, Father Patrick Skehan. It shows part of the Song of Moses in Deuteronomy 32, and from the appearance of the manuscript it appears that this song had once a separate circulation with arrangement of the text in hemistichs, a characteristic also of some canonical Psalm manuscripts from Qumran. Such a freedom in the treatment of the Law would have horrified a later copyist but appears to be nothing unusual among the Qumran scribes. Here again is a three-column arrangement of my translation of the latter part of Skehan's reconstructed text, together with the LXX and Revised Version.

QUMRAN	LXX	RV
Deuteronomy xxxii. 41–3 I will render venge[ance to] mine adversaries, [and] will recompense them [that hate] me. [I will make] mine arrows [drunk] with blood, [and my sword shall devou]r flesh; [with the blood of the slain and] the captives, from [the head] of the l[eader]s of the enemy. Rejoice, O ye heavens, with him and all ye gods worship him; for he will avenge the blood of his sons and will render vengeance to his adversaries, and will reward them that hate him; and will make expiation for the land of his people.	and will render vengeance to mine adversaries, and will recompense them that hate me. I will make my weapons drunk with blood, and my sword shall devour flesh; with the blood of the slain and the captives, from the head of the leaders of the enemies. Rejoice, O ye heavens, with him and let all the angels of God worship him; Rejoice, O ye nations with his people, and let all the sons of God accord him strength; for he will avenge the blood of his sons, and will render vengeance and recompense justice to his adversaries, and will reward them that hate him; and the Lord will make expiation for the land of his people.	I will render vengeance to mine adversaries, and will recompense them that hate me. I will make mine arrows drunk with blood, and my sword shall devour flesh; with the blood of the slain and the captives, from the head of the leaders of the enemy. Rejoice, O ye nations, with his people; for he will avenge the blood of his servants, and will render vengeance to his adversaries, and will make expiation for his land, for his people.

Thus, in these small fragments, with no more than forty complete or near-complete words of the Hebrew text remaining, we are able to confirm the existence of another divergent Hebrew text with strong affinities to the Hebrew recension underlying the LXX. From the above the reader will be able to notice some of the principles upon which the LXX translators worked, here a conflation, there a slight alteration to avoid giving offence, as in its rendering of 'all ye gods', as 'all ye angels of God'. MT avoids all reference to these heavenly creatures with 'all ye nations'.

Another version which has been used, with some caution, for textual criticism is that cherished by the small Samaritan community living at Nablus in Jordan, near ancient Shechem. It contains only the Pentateuch written in a formalized and rather artificially developed imitation of the ancient palaeo-Hebrew script. The earliest manuscript hitherto known was that at present in the hands of the community and written probably in the eleventh century of our era, although the community itself believes that it dates from the time of Moses! Knowledge of this tradition in Western scholarship is comparatively late, the first copy coming to light in the seventeenth century. There followed a spirited debate on the value of the version as an independent authority for the text of the Pentateuch, until Gesenius in 1815 pronounced against the Samaritan version, maintaining that it was clearly secondary and offered hardly a single reading which was preferable to MT. It differs in about 6,000 places, but most are orthographic or syntactic differences, whilst others are supplements to correct apparent deficiencies in the text with the help of similar passages in other books, repetitions of speeches and the like from parallel passages, the removal of obscurities, and the insertion of explanatory glosses. It could often be shown that differences in matters of substance owed their origin to the dogmatic arguments of this Jewish sect, and could not therefore be regarded as original. But despite this, it was undeniable that here and there the Samaritan version did preserve some better readings, and it was not insignificant that of the 6,000 differences, 1,900 agree with LXX against MT. For example, in Exodus xii. 40, the 430 years of sojourning is said to have been in Canaan as well as Egypt, as in LXX (compare Galatians iii. 17). In Genesis iv. 8,

> And Cain said to Abel his brother, *Let us go into the field,*

is read by the Samaritan with LXX and other versions, and similarly in Genesis xv. 21, it gives

> and the Girgashite, *and the Hivite,* and the Jebusite,

with LXX; in Genesis xxi. 13,

> also of the son of the bondwoman will I make a *great* nation,

as LXX and other versions; in Genesis xvii. 14,

> not circumcised in the flesh of his foreskin *on the eighth day,*

again in accordance with LXX and other versions.

These traces of genuine alternative traditions to MT made scholars hesitate before condemning the Samaritan version as late and comparatively worthless, and now Qumran has given it a remarkable vindication; for from the Fourth Cave have come fragments of the Pentateuch, written in a palaeo-Hebrew script whose texts correspond in all essential points with the Samaritan version. Father Skehan has published a preliminary account of such a text of Exodus. In it, Exodus vii. 18 is followed by the beginning of the fulfilment by Moses of the command given him in vii. 16–18, which in the Samaritan version is repeated almost completely. Similarly, vii. 29 is followed by 'and he came' in the Qumran fragment, and is clearly the beginning of the Samaritan expansion which related the fulfilment of the command given in vii. 26–9. Exodus viii. 19 is again followed by an expansion which records the carrying out of viii. 16–19, and similarly again at ix. 5 and ix. 19 fulfilling the commands of ix. 1–5 and ix. 13–19 respectively. Exodus xi. 2 is followed, as again in the Samaritan text, by an ex-

pansion which anticipates most of verses 4–7. In Exodus
xvii. 13, Samaritan and Qumran add, after 'his people',
'and he smote them'. Just as in Samaritan, expansions from
Deuteronomy have been introduced into the Qumran
scroll, and the Samaritan omissions of Exodus xxix. 21 and
xxx. 1–10 are reproduced here also.

What this means, in effect, is that the Samaritan community have preserved a recension dating, presumably,
from the time of the establishment of their own centre in the
fifth century B.C., and which at least from the second
century has remained virtually intact. However, as Skehan
points out in his article, this does not change the overwhelming impression that it gives of being a secondary
version. Thus its deficiencies, its free treatment of the text
by additions and transpositions, must be recognized before
it is used as evidence against MT. Nevertheless where it
does show a better text its evidence must be given full
weight, particularly where its support by the Greek shows
it to have retained an earlier tradition than that of MT.
In fact, once more, each case must be decided on its merits,
and the Samaritan given the authority of a very early recension. A further incidental question which will have to be
reconsidered is the use by a strict Jewish sect like that of
Qumran of a recension which had been adopted two centuries or more before by the heretical Samaritans. Indeed,
this is by no means the only link between Qumran and the
Samaritan community, and is a question which offers a
challenging field of research.

But it should not be imagined that the Qumran biblical
texts follow necessarily any one of the versions consistently.
Although this seems to be so in the case of this palaeo-
Hebrew Exodus manuscript, we have seen that Samuel
varies somewhat in this respect and other manuscripts of
Exodus and of other books of the Bible seem often to
show a 'mixed' tradition. For example, another Exodus
text gives marked LXX readings, as in i. 5 where MT
reads:

And all the souls that came out of the loins of Jacob were seventy souls: and Joseph was in Egypt already. And Joseph died . . .

and our new text, with LXX, has

. . . seventy-five souls. And [Joseph] died . . .

(cp. Acts vii. 14, etc.). On the other hand, other Exodus texts give readings which correspond now with LXX and now with Samaritan, and sometimes with neither. Similarly one well-represented Numbers manuscript shows an extraordinary text which goes with Samaritan, LXX, and MT in turn, and is further characterized with rubric written very neatly in red ink. A typical Samaritan reading is the insertion from Deuteronomy iii. 21 in Numbers xxvii. 23.

[and he sai]d to him, Thine eyes have seen all that the Lord hath done to [these] two k[ings].

Yet in xxxv. 21 after 'he is a manslayer', Qumran has

the slayer shall surely be put to death

exactly as in LXX, but against the Samaritan and MT. Then, again, two manuscripts of Joshua show marked LXX readings, whilst, coming into the prophetic texts, copies of Jeremiah show again a mixed text which will require further study to clarify. There are three relatively well preserved manuscripts of the book of Daniel, and the text seems to conform in most places with MT, preserving the transition from Aramaic to Hebrew in precisely the same place. However there are a few rare variants agreeing with the Alexandrian LXX against MT and Theodotion.

The overall picture, then, of the biblical texts possessed by this Community seems to be one of complete freedom of choice. They were not, like their later brethren, limited to any one text tradition, a state of affairs which, interestingly enough, obtains at Murabba'at sixty years later, where all the biblical texts found keep rigidly to the Massoretic tradition. Yet, even at Qumran, it can hardly be doubted that the MT type was gaining ground by its intrinsic merit, and it is certainly well represented among the biblical fragments from the Fourth Cave as well as the Isaiah scrolls from the First. It was never inviolate, however. Changes from its prototype have certainly been introduced over the centuries of its transmission, whether from slips of the pen or deliberate alterations to smooth over inherited difficulties in the reading, or even to introduce readings more in conformity with the theological standpoint of the time. Sometimes in Qumran fragments we have a variant reading of a difficult passage which offers nothing in clarification over MT but at least shows that both texts found the same difficulty and tackled it in different ways. All this demonstrates that, although the standard text of our Bible is certainly very old and very reliable, it has not been without some scribal errors and 'adjustment' which will not allow for it any false claims of 'originality'.

How, then, is the new evidence from Qumran going to affect our Bible translations? It is, of course, early yet to come to any detailed conclusions, but certain fundamental principles seem inescapable. Whilst the versions have, from the very beginning of scientific textual criticism, been given their full weight by scholars in determining a more original text, it has always been the tradition in Protestant circles to base the popular translations on the Hebrew standard version, or Massoretic Text, on the sound principle that it alone is the most fully preserved text in the original tongue. Whilst the Greek may offer here and there a better reading, its origins were always dubious, since we knew very little about the nature of the Hebrew text before the translators, or indeed if, in these cases, it really existed in a different form from MT, and the better reading were not merely the arbitrary emendation of the translator. Thus a Greek reading, even if clearly preferable for the sense of the passage, was usually consigned to the margin, on the primary principle that at all costs, even, all too often, of Hebrew grammar and lexicography, the standard text must be made to give sense. Only if all else failed and still no possible translation could be squeezed from the Hebrew were the

Plate 1. Muhammad's Cave (One).

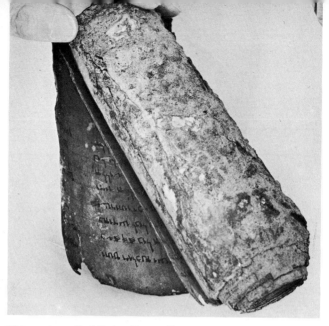

Plate 2a. A scroll of Psalms from a Qumran cave.

Plate 2b. Joseph Saad in the grounds of the Palestine Archaeological Museum, Jerusalem.

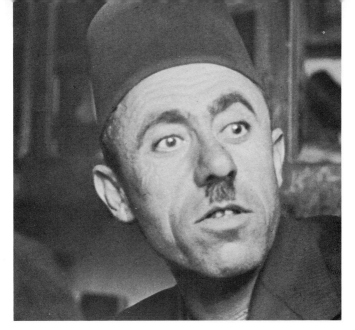

Plate 3a. Kando.

Plate 3b. The main street, Bethlehem. Kando's cobbler's shop is among the shops across the road.

Plate 4a. Caves Four and Five, Qumran.

Plate 4b. Inside Cave Four (the 'Cave of the Wounded Partridge').

Plate 5a. Bedouin at work in a cave near the
Dead Sea.

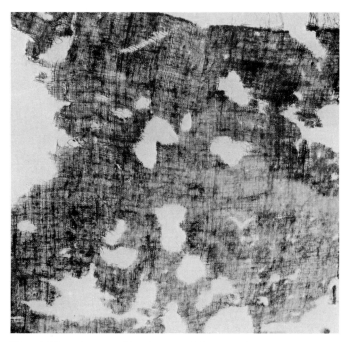

Plate 5b. Linen from the First Cave, used for wrapping the
Scrolls.

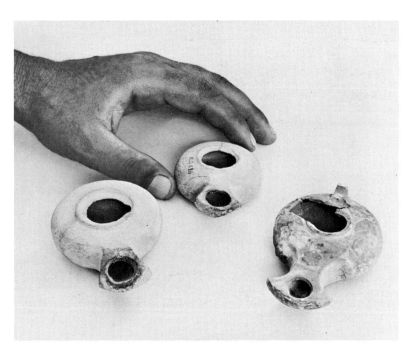

Plate 6a. Roman period lamps from Qumran.

Plate 6b. An axe or mattock from a Qumran cave.

Plate 7a. Items from the Chalcolithic Period (4–3,000 B.C.) of the Murabba'at caves, including a wooden adze handle, complete with its leather thongs for fastening the flint blade.

Plate 7b. Part of a leather sandal from Murabba'at, probably from the Middle Bronze Period, *c.* 2,000 B.C.

Plate 8a. An alphabet painted on to a broken potsherd, perhaps by an apprentice scribe.

Plate 8b. A coin of Simon bar Kochebah (the abbreviation *sh-m-ʿ* (for *shimʿôn*, Simon) is written around the trunk of the palm tree).

Plate 8c. Part of the treasure hoard of silver coins, found buried under the floor of one of the monastery rooms, Qumran.

Plate 9. Gerald Lankester Harding, a visitor, and Father Milik at Khirbet Qumran.

Plate 10a. Part of the Jerusalem 'Scrollery'.

Plate 10b. Newly purchased scroll fragments being sorted on arrival in the 'Scrollery'.

Plate 11a. The author at work on a Qumran commentary on Nahum.

Plate 11b. A papyrus palimpsest inscribed in Hebrew letters of about the eighth century B.C.

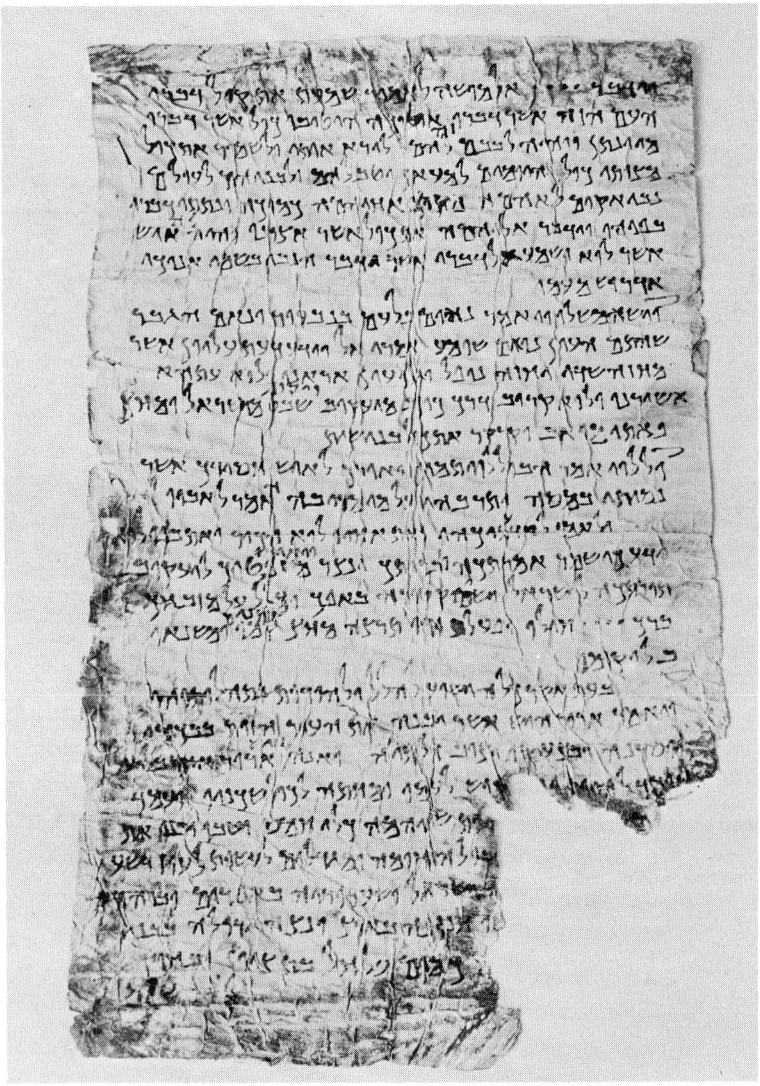

Plate 12. The Testimonia document from the Fourth Cave.

renderings of the versions allowed to take their place in the text of the translation. It seems now that, to scholars engaged on this work in the future, Qumran has offered a new basis for a confidence in the LXX in at least the historical books, which should allow them to accept the better readings of that version almost as readily as if they were found in the Hebrew MT. In other words, each reading must in future be judged *on its merits*, not on any preconceived notion of the superiority of the Hebrew version, simply because it is Hebrew. If the Greek offers a better reading, then that ought to be taken and put in the text of the translation; if the Samaritan recension gives better sense, then that ought to be given first place, since we now know that it has at least as great a claim to antiquity as the Qumran exemplars of MT. This gives support to those scholars who would make an eclectic text the foundation of a future translation. The whole business becomes infinitely more complicated, and, it must be admitted, more subjective. And that is the difficulty. To make such an eclectic version demands the use of critical faculties on the traditions which many scholars would hesitate to employ on a popular version. They will say, with much justice, that to make a choice between two or more readings in a sacred text is a responsibility which no body of men ought to be asked to make, or even that it is possible to make with any hope of permanence. They will point, for instance, to the text criticism of only a few decades ago when the fashion in scholarship was then to regard as hopelessly out-of-date and reactionary the practice of leaving two verses standing together, or to do anything else with a corrupt text than to rip it out entirely and rewrite it as they themselves would have done had they been the author. Fashions in textual criticism change as in most other things, and little permanence could be expected from a Bible translation which depended so much on the personal preferences of a few scholars of a certain age. No sooner was one translation ready for the press than a new set of translators would want to begin another.

This is all perfectly true, but the choice seems to be

between offering to the public as perfect a rendering as possible of an imperfect text merely because it happens to be the one complete Hebrew recension of the Bible we possess, and between using every faculty of modern scholarship to compose a version which, if it can make no claim to infallibility, at least has the merit of treating all the difficulties of the text seriously, glossing none over with impossible renderings in italics or otherwise, and making full use of ancient versions whose Hebrew originals we now know to have existed, and parts of which we actually have in our possession. The one way is safer for the scholar involved, since he can defend all his readings by reference to only one text, and he cuts down the area of subjective judgement to a minimum. To attempt the other is to invite continual accusations of partisanship and over-subjectivity in a matter which for very many people is a matter of personal faith. On the other hand, the cry for permanence in a Bible translation is a vain one these days. Hardly a day passes without some new light being thrown upon the meanings of the text of the Bible: new inscriptions are found or deciphered, archaeological excavations give us a better idea of how the people of those days lived, and all this affects our understanding of the text. We can never expect any translation now to be accorded the long-lived and undeserved authority of the King James version. Similarly, the cry for objectivity is just as misplaced. Scholars are only human, and translations, from one language to another, despite the new electronic translation machines, are among the most subjective of man's activities. It is true that to widen the field of translation to more than one text is to risk more subjectivity in the answer, but the question is only one of degree. The public, one presumes, is more interested in having a translation which is as near as possible what the prophet spoke or wrote than an accurate rendering of a particular Hebrew manuscript. If Qumran helps us to satisfy that requirement, then I believe we should use all the information it can offer, even though it makes our work vastly more complicated.

In any case, the whole question must be seen in a proper sense of proportion. The comparative translations which have been given in the previous pages will make it clear to the reader that to use another translation is not going to change the whole face of our Bible. The differences are matters of detail and should result in a clearer, smoother text than the one we have been wont to use. And again, the principle of an eclectic text is not so strange. We have recently seen a very good example of what can be done in this way in the translation of the Scriptures offered by the Catholic Biblical Association of America. Here all the versions have been accorded full weight of authority and their readings, where clearly preferable, included in the text, whilst separate sections give full textual notes wherever the versions have been used in place of the Hebrew. The result is not only extremely readable, but a major work of scholarly erudition which might well be a model of future translations, whose collaborators will now have the support of the new Qumran material to give them confidence in their use of other recensions.

CHAPTER FIVE

THE EXCAVATIONS AT QUMRAN

The First Cave

THERE is a hotel at the north end of the Dead Sea that proclaims itself 'the lowest place on earth'. This is literally quite true, for the surface of the Dead Sea lies some 1,300 feet below normal sea-level. It is at the end of the Jordan Rift Valley which continues southwards into Africa. On either side of the Dead Sea, limestone cliffs form the sides of a basin into which the sun pours for most of the year, and which lies in an almost totally effective rain-shadow.

The Sea's only outlet is evaporation under the scorching sun, and its main replenishment comes from the fast-diminishing waters of the River Jordan at its northern end.

The outlet of the Wady Qumran lies about five miles down the western side of the Sea. Walking inland from the shore at this point, the visitor crosses a mile or so of salty scrub land before reaching the edge of the marly plateau on which the Qumran ruins stand. Behind these are the cliffs themselves, rising in stages to a plateau at about normal sea-level.

Muhammad's cave (pl. 1) is to be found about a thousand yards north of Khirbet Qumran, at the top of the first stage of rocky ascent from the plateau. Although the site is fast becoming one of Jordan's main tourist attractions, the visitor may rest assured that it will be many years before he will be besieged by postcard-selling guides and ice-cream vendors. The area is completely barren, and although cars can reach the foot of the cliffs, from then on the visitor must climb the steep slopes on foot, and the sharp-edged limestone rocks are unkind to the hardiest shoes. The loose shale also makes the climb difficult, and parties should keep together at the worst parts to help each other where the going becomes treacherous. However, the climb is not impossible for the most sedentary tourist, though he will almost certainly need a guide to find the right spot to begin the climb. Failing this, he may be aided by the knowledge that, after crossing the first main wady north of Qumran, keeping to the track which runs beneath the cliffs, he will come upon the circles of stones marking the site of the camp of the 1949 excavators. A little farther on he will note on his right a large boulder standing on its own in the plain, and looking towards the left he will see another at the foot of the cliffs. Taking a bearing through these stones, he will be led to the heap of tumbled shale which is the beginning of the climb. If he keeps going straight up from here he cannot miss the cave on his right, behind a pinnacle of rock. Entrance can now be made easily through the narrow vertical opening enlarged by the clandestine excavators, and above can be seen the hole through which the Bedouin lad threw the stone. Inside, of course, the floor has been completely turned over, but otherwise the cave differs little from how it must have looked in 1947 when Muhammad lost his goat.

Official excavations, under the leadership of Mr Lankester Harding, and Father De Vaux of the French School of Archaeology in Jerusalem, began on 15 February 1949 and continued until 5 March. First to be examined was the dump left by the clandestine diggers, and this yielded large quantities of sherds and linen scroll wrappings (pl. 5b), and a few pieces of inscribed leather, including the first fragment recovered from Qumran written in the old proto-Hebraic or 'Phoenician' characters, and representing part of the text of Leviticus. The filling of the cave itself consisted of a fine powdery dust, and stones fallen from the sides and roof of the cave. Every ounce of this material had to be minutely examined with nothing more mechanical than a pair of tweezers and a camel-hair brush, for the slightest pressure will often break the scroll fragments even further, and, being covered with this marly deposit, they are easily missed amongst the debris.

The documentary results of this exacting toil produced hundreds of pieces, ranging in size from those smaller than a fingernail to fragments containing several lines of writing. As they were found, the pieces were carefully placed between glass plates and taken to the Jerusalem Museum for photographing. A part of a scroll, now completely coagulated with damp into a mass of glue, was found adhering to the collar of a broken jar, and still covered with its linen wrapper. Small leather phylactery cases were found, made in two parts stitched together, forming four small pouches into which minute rolls of very fine parchment had once been placed. These, inscribed with certain portions of the Old Testament, were believed to act as a sort of charm for the wearer. Single compartment phylacteries were also found, and, among the fragments, the remains of a phylactery itself, though from its size unlikely to have belonged to any of the cases found. Two fragments of a wooden comb were also found, which seem to indicate that perhaps this cave was anciently used for a dwelling place as well as a deposit for the library.

By this time all the intact jars had been taken away or broken. Professor Sukenik had purchased two from Kando, and I myself bought another from him in 1953 which was quite intact, apart from a small hole near the bottom sealed with pitch. Some of the sherds recovered showed signs of recent breakage, probably received during the clandestine pillage, but patient work in the Museum restored many jars to their original shape, and some were later sold to museums all over the world. Other pieces of pottery included the parts of several bowl-like jar lids, some bowls, a cooking-pot, a small jug, and several lamps.

The scroll jars themselves came to assume a magnified importance for the archaeologists, who were particularly concerned at this stage in finding some criteria by which the cave deposit might be dated. The difficulty was that the jars were practically unique in shape and size. Generally between 21 in. and 27 in. long, they were cylindrical in shape, flattening sharply at top and bottom to a wide collared neck and ring base respectively. Marks of turning are clearly visible on the sides, and the deep firing has given the pottery a hard, almost metallic quality, with a characteristic rose-pink or grey colouring. Some of the jars vary somewhat from this general pattern, being smaller and with rather more bulging sides, whilst one has a rounded bottom. Another characteristic of the smaller jars are the handles on the shoulders, sometimes small and vertical like those of a cup, but other times nothing more than horizontal lugs, pierced with holes through which string could be passed to retain the lid in position. When at a later date such smaller jars were found in the ruins of the Settlement itself, it was realized that they must have been storage jars, and thus not necessarily used for preserving written documents, so that it could no longer be maintained that all the forty or fifty vessels found represented in the First Cave were essentially 'scroll jars'.

The nearest parallel to the characteristic large jars of Qumran is certainly to be seen in vessels found in Egypt at the beginning of this century and similarly containing documentary material which could be dated to the second century B.C. It is not improbable, therefore, that the general shape of the jars and idea of scroll storage were borrowed by the Qumran sect from Egypt, and this is by no means the only indication of a fairly close contact between it and that area. But certainly for Palestinian ceramics these jars were unique. However, the other pottery found in the cave could be matched with discoveries made elsewhere in the country. The cooking-pot and the narrow-necked juglet were closely similar to those found in Jewish tombs in the environs of Jerusalem and elsewhere, dating to late Hellenistic or Roman times, i.e., from the first half of the first century B.C. down to the fall of Jerusalem in A.D.70. Two of the lamps seemed to be Hellenistic in general appearance, but another couple were certainly no earlier than Roman (pl. 6a). At first this was interpreted by the archaeologists as pointing to a Hellenistic date for the deposit with a later Roman entry. However, after excavations had been made on the ruined

Settlement itself, where more jars were found and where coins gave a final dating for the main period of occupation to A.D. 68, it was conceded that the early dating of the cave was probably wrong, and the deposit there would have to be brought down also to Roman times. The earlier types of the lamps must then be attributed to later copying. Now that we have been able to examine the palaeographical evidence afforded by the remains of hundreds more scrolls from other caves in the area, everything seems to substantiate this dating, and certainly none of the literary evidence so far obtained from the fragments militates against it.

The practice of putting scrolls in jars for safe storage was by no means uncommon in antiquity, and in his report on the archaeology of the First Cave, Father De Vaux recalls instances ranging from the time of Rameses III down to an Arab letter of the eighth or ninth century of our era where the practice is referred to. Unfortunately our Qumran community did not always use this admirable method, and in other caves the scrolls had been left without such protection, so that they have deteriorated to fragments by the ravaging of animals and the elements. Why the Sectarians should have put some into jars and left others without adequate protection is a puzzle. The answer probably is that some had been put away properly with a view to their preservation and perhaps future use, whilst others had been thrown into the nearest hiding-place available at the approach of the enemy who finally forced them to flee. But it seems not improbable that some of the caves where fragments were found had been dwelling-places of members of the Sect, who had left their own private copies of the Scriptures in them, and abandoned them at the last moment, perhaps because they had no time to return to their caves.

The puzzle of the uniqueness of the jars in Palestine was solved when the archaeologists found in the ruins of the Settlement a pottery kiln (pl. 18), showing that in this, as in many other things, the Sect tried to be as independent of the outside world as possible. Working to Egyptian patterns they had probably adapted them to their own use and thus produced a type of pottery which could not be paralleled elsewhere in Palestine.

The flaxen scroll coverings recovered from the cave (pl. 5b) were sent to the late Mrs G. M. Crowfoot for expert examination, and her report in the Cave One volume of *Discoveries in the Judaean Desert* makes interesting reading. All the fragments appear to have come from small cloths, definitely shaped and sewn. Some were certainly designed as scroll wrappers, while others had been folded into pads and may have formed a packing for the scrolls inside the jars. Other pieces were found with twisted corners tied with string, and doubtless served as jar covers tied across the open necks. Some of the cloths were decorated with blue lines, and the Shirley Institute of Manchester found, on examination, that the dye used was certainly indigo. The usual form of decoration consists of simple blue lines in the weft, generally of two wefts only, although, in the case of one piece, the weft is double, and, on another, an embroidered line is added. There was only one piece found with a more elaborate pattern complete, a design of rectangles within one another, but there is evidence that this design was attempted on other less well-preserved cloths. Jewish writings give ample evidence for the working of flax between the second century B.C. and the second A.D. in Palestine, and Mrs Crowfoot's conclusion was that the linen of the scroll cave was a local product. Although in some respects, rather as the scroll jars do, it shows similarities with the Egyptian variety, there are essential differences which give it a rather more coarse appearance. By a very careful examination of the materials, Mrs Crowfoot also hazarded the opinion that the loom used was a rather primitive, warp-weighted upright structure, although the type with an upper and lower beam was probably in use at this time in Palestine as elsewhere.

Another interesting examination of the flaxen textiles was carried out, this time in the laboratories of the University of Chicago, by Dr W. F. Libby. The object of these experiments was the determination by radiological means of the date at which the flax was cut. This almost incredible possibility was made feasible by the discovery that an atomically unstable form of carbon, whose atomic weight is 14 instead of the normal 12, was continually being created in the earth's upper atmosphere by the bombardment of cosmic rays on Nitrogen-14 atoms. The resultant Carbon-14 combines with oxygen to make a particular form of carbon dioxide, which becomes mixed with normal carbon dioxide in definite proportions. Thus Carbon-14 is breathed by all living plants and animals in their various life processes, and as a result, as Libby showed in 1946, all such creatures contain a constant proportion of the unstable Carbon-14, in the proportion of about one trillionth of a gram of Carbon-14 to one gram of Carbon-12. With death, of course, the intake of Carbon-14 comes to an end, but the amount in the body remains and slowly disintegrates at a constant rate. The 'half-life' of Carbon-14 is 5,568 years, so that one ounce would become half an ounce in that length of time, a quarter of an ounce in the next 5,568 years, and so on. It will be clear that if the amount remaining in a specimen of organic matter can be accurately measured, the time since it ceased to breathe this heavy form of carbon can be estimated without difficulty. The laboratory procedure is to burn the sample to pure carbon, and then measure the residue with an extremely sensitive radiation meter on the Geiger-counter principle. The measurement is expressed in terms of the number of Carbon-14 disintegrations per minute per gram of carbon. This value is 15.3 for a contemporary living sample, 7.65 for a sample 5,568 years old, 3.83 for a sample 11,136 years old, and so on. But it is not surprising to know that in calculating such infinitesimal quantities a margin of error must be allowed for which increases with the age of the sample. The acknowledged error is between 5 and 10 per cent, and the limit of measurable range, 20,000 years. It seems likely, however, that new methods will cut the margin of error considerably and increase the range. Although Carbon-14 is present in all organic matter, it appears that certain kinds of material have been found most amenable to the test, such as plant-growth like wood and charcoal, shell, antler and burned bone, dung, and peat. Tests made on material which can be otherwise dated have brought some amazingly accurate results. A slab of wood from the roof beam of an Egyptian vizier's house of the First Dynasty, variously dated between 3100 and 2800 B.C. averaged, over two 'runs', 2,933 with a margin of error of 200 years, and a piece of deck planking from the funeral boat of King Sesostris III, who died about 1849 B.C., gave a reading which brought this date well within the marginal errors. It was thus with some excitement that the results from the flaxen scroll covers of the First Cave were awaited. Dr Libby announced that from his calculations the flax used in the material was cut in A.D. 33, with a margin of error of plus or minus 200 years, i.e. within the range A.D. 233 and 168 B.C. (there being of course, no year '0'). So near is this central date for what, on other evidence, must be the time of the preparation of the cloths, that the result is almost breathtaking, and opens up a wonderful prospect of accuracy in archaeological dating of the future.

The ink used on the scrolls was tested in the British Museum research laboratories by Dr H. J. Plenderleith, who found it to be of a carbon composition resistant to mild bleaching and, one may add, to a surprising amount of hard brushing which attempts at reading and matching have made necessary at times. There has been very little fading of the writing on the fragments, and in many cases it stands out as freshly as the day it was written.

The skin of the fragments was tested in the Department of Leather Industries, as it was then called, of the University of Leeds, to whose Director at the time, Dr Donald Burton, a box of blank samples was sent for expert examination. The nature of the skins and the grouping of the hair follicles indicated young goats and lambs as the main source of the material, which would not rule out the possibility that the Qumran community were preparing their own writing materials. But there was no trace of tanning agents, and a close examination of the fibres under an electron microscope of 25,000× magnification revealed a condition of the skin exactly paralleled in parchment. To judge from these samples, therefore, we should refer to these scrolls as parchment rather than leather.

Another test on the skins made by the Leeds laboratories was designed to establish their age by a shrinkage-temperature process. It had been shown that the older a piece of skin was the lower the temperature at which it began to shrink. A tiny piece of the sample is teased out in distilled water which is then electrically heated under controlled conditions. The temperature at which the fibres begin to shrink, as viewed under a microscope, is carefully noted and compared with results obtained from other dated samples. At present these tests can only give a relative dating, and, of course, one difficulty has been to find skins of comparable antiquity with that of the scrolls and which can be accurately dated. However, the tests against ancient Egyptian samples and pieces of medieval bookbinding, for instance, showed conclusively that the scroll fragments were far older than the latter, and gave no support at all to those few scholars who were still maintaining in face of all the evidence that the scrolls were medieval.

The Monastery

During the excavations of the cave in the early spring of 1949, De Vaux and Harding had naturally looked around for some evidence of human habitation nearby which might be connected with the deposit of scrolls. About a thousand yards to the SSE. of the first cave they discovered the ruins of Khirbet Qumran (pl. 16a and map on p. 9), which had already been seen before by travellers and mentioned in their reports. De Saulcy, in 1851, had suggested they might be the remains of the biblical Gomorrah, which must surely have made our pious Sectarians turn in their graves. The first valuable description was given by Clermont Ganneau in 1873, and Dalman correctly recognized Roman remains on the spot in his report of 1920. But the ruins remained virtually untouched until Harding and De Vaux decided to make a trial sounding in 1949, and dug out two of the tombs in the adjacent cemetery (pl. 19). This extends to the east of the ruins and contains about a thousand graves, nearly all of which were orientated north and south. This fact is very strange in a Muslim country, and Clermont Ganneau had commented on the peculiarity, suggesting that they must date from pre-Islamic times. They are marked by a simple oval of stones, with an occasional dressed stone at the extremities, and when excavated proved to be of extremely simple construction, with practically no grave furniture at all. A shaft had been dug through the pebbles of the marine terrace and through the marl below to a depth which varied between four and six feet. At the bottom, the grave itself had been dug usually into the eastern side and then covered with crude bricks of unburnt clay or simply stones. The body had been extended on its back, head to the south, the hands crossed above the pelvis or at the sides. The absence of any of the ornamentation or personal jewellery one might have expected in these graves, confirmed the impression of strict discipline and communal living which the first thorough excavations of the ruins themselves also gave. For when, at the end of 1951, the rubble was cleared from the walls, and the main outlines of the building stood out, it was seen that this could be no dwelling-house, but some sort of monastery, having large meeting rooms with plaster benches running round the walls, and outside the main building a large water cistern (pl. 21) far beyond the needs of an ordinary family. One of the most important of the objects found amongst the ruins was an intact jar of exactly the same shape as those found in the First Cave, thus linking quite certainly the cave and the ruins, the scrolls and the people who had inhabited the Settlement and had been buried in the cemetery. Some evidence of the nature of the destruction of the buildings was found when, in clearing away the surface debris, the excavators came upon a layer of black powder covered with a coating of marl. Careful clearing of the latter revealed the unmistakable remains of charred reeds, and here and there

93

below these, blackened palm trunks. These were clearly the remains of reed roofs laid across palm timbers and plastered with marl in exactly the same fashion as houses are roofed in Jericho today. Indeed only a few hundred yards from the ruins the visitor may see a watchman's hut roofed in precisely the same manner. A fire had destroyed the buildings in antiquity, as the charring showed all too clearly, and the presence of iron arrow heads found later in the rooms confirmed the impression of a violent end to the Community.

Gradually the excavator's craft was filling in the outline of the life of these people who had bequeathed to mankind such an amazing legacy of priceless manuscripts. But the second and later seasons were to broaden our knowledge still further; for the Settlement seems to have had a complicated history, whose discernment from the maze of walls and water conduits (pl. 20) of the ruins has taxed all the powers of scholarship and resourcefulness of the archaeologists concerned.

With the help of about two hundred and fifty coins found amid the ruins it was possible to sketch out three main periods in the constructional history of Khirbet Qumran, the first two being separated by a period beginning with a violent earthquake. Indeed, the latest excavations make it appear that its history may go back even before the Roman period into the Iron Age, but this cannot be our immediate concern. As far as the Sect is concerned, building seems to have started in or fairly soon after the reign of John Hyrcanus (135–104 B.C.), from which the first important batch of coins found in the ruins come, and the series carry on in an unbroken succession until the time of Herod the Great (37–4 B.C.). Only ten of his coins have been found, and the series begins again from Herod Archelaus (4 B.C.– A.D. 6) and continues until the third year of the First Revolt (beginning in the spring of A.D. 68) and the main destruction by fire. There are a handful of Roman coins contemporaneous with this, produced at Caesarea and Dora. Here the Roman emperors minted coins for the provinces and the legions, so they may be assumed to be from the pay packets of Roman legionaries stationed at Qumran after its destruction. The next large batch are of the Second Jewish Revolt of A.D. 132–5.

By a stroke of good fortune it is possible to make another pivotal dating in the history of the Settlement, since the earthquake which seems to have brought the first occupational period to an end can be accurately dated. From the historian, Flavius Josephus, writing in the first century of our era, we learn that in the spring of 31 B.C. a terrible earthquake shook Judaea, devastating its towns and killing thousands of men and beasts. It happened in the seventh year of Herod the Great, when he was actively engaged against the Nabateans. The earthquake, we are told, so terrified his men, encamped in the plains of Jericho, that he had difficulty in exhorting them to courage in the face of the enemy. It was most probably this shock which caused the crack in the cistern shown in plate 21 and which ran right through the adjoining cistern and room leaving a subsidence of 20 inches or so to the east of this line. In the NW. tower, the eastern wall is split, and the lintel of the door between two of the rooms is broken, causing the ceiling of one to collapse. On the walls S. and E. of this room, the plaster is cracked in two lines converging on the SE. corner. Clearly all this damage points to a violent shaking of the earth, and the evidence of the coins would point to the beginning of Herod's reign for its occurrence, which fits well with Josephus' earthquake of 31 B.C. But one question still awaits a definite answer: Did the earthquake drive out the inhabitants or had they already left when it occurred? One can understand their being frightened at the time, and scurrying out of the buildings, but they could easily retire to their caves or tents and come back later to clear up the mess. Yet apparently they did not rebuild the Settlement for something like thirty years, until after Herod had died. If that king had anything to do with their retirement from Qumran, then they would probably have gone before the earthquake in 31 B.C., since he had by then been ruling for seven years. But that raises a difficulty, for if, as now seems probable, this sect is to be identified with a party of the Essenes, Josephus tells us that Herod was favourably inclined towards them because one of their number had once given a favourable prognostication regarding certain of his activities. On the other hand, it is doubtful whether this would have stopped him clearing them out of Qumran if he had felt that their presence on his frontiers was a menace to security.

In any case the Sectarians seem to have returned in force after his death and cleared out the rubble from the buildings and rebuilt the walls. A trench, sunk on the north side by the excavators, cut through one of the rubbish dumps made at this time, and brought to light whole and broken pottery and a few coins, as well as the rubble of stone and plaster from the broken walls. This second period then lasted until the fall of the monastery in A.D. 68. At this point again we have some welcome confirmatory evidence from Josephus, who tells us that, in the late spring of this year, the emperor Vespasian brought his Tenth Legion down the Jordan Valley to Jericho. Hearing strange stories about the wonderful buoyancy of the Dead Sea he had the hands of several non-swimmers tied behind their backs and threw them into the water. Sure enough they floated, but one hopes for their sakes that they kept their eyes shut against the salt-saturated water or they might well have wished they had not. We are told that Vespasian left a garrison at Jericho, and two years later Titus led the Legion against Jerusalem to raze that city to the ground.

It is possible that the Sectarians of Qumran did not stay to the bitter end, but deposited their precious scrolls against their return and then hastened away before it was too late. Josephus tells us that the Roman approach was heralded by a general panic, when the mass of the population fled into 'those mountainous parts which lay over against Jerusalem'. The presence of the arrow heads among the debris certainly points to some resistance from the buildings, but since the Zealots were certainly active in Masada and En

Geddi to the south, it is not impossible that it was they who took over the defence of this strategic position commanding the way to the south and offering a perfect look-out to the head of the Dead Sea. It may have been their defence which the Romans avenged with fire and sword.

The victors did not leave immediately, and the third period in the life of the buildings is marked by a re-utilization of its defence works, the levelling of the debris to some extent, and the division of the larger meeting rooms into small living quarters. They enlarged the bread oven which had been built towards the end of the last Sectarian occupation, and made changes in the water conduits to serve their practical needs of mere physical existence. The large cisterns were no longer used, which points to a much smaller group of inhabitants without the Sect's ritualistic requirement for water. After a time these too left, and the place remained empty until, in the time of the Second Revolt, the Jewish guerrilla forces made use of the monastery's excellent strategic position for a strong point protecting the Dead Sea route to their southern posts. When they too withdrew, the desert took possession of its own, and save for the occasional wandering shepherd none came to break its peace or recall the glories of its past, until Muhammad Adh-Dhib lost his goat one summer's day in 1947.

Now, thanks to the skilful work of Harding and De Vaux and their teams, the visitor can walk again through the rooms and passages of the monastery. It may be of interest to describe in detail some of the more interesting characteristics of the building.

The walls stand highest at the NW. corner which contains the watch-tower already mentioned. Here they are some four or five feet thick, and the lower stage contains rooms which communicate with each other but not externally. They give the impression of a closely guarded storehouse, or even prison cells. A spiral staircase originally communicated with the upper stage, and its central pillar is still to be seen in one of the lower rooms. On the higher stage of the tower were three rooms with a door to the outside facing south. But this door was accessible only by means of a ladder, or, perhaps, a wooden gallery running along the west wall as far as a staircase, whose remains are visible a few yards to the south. Two open passages surrounding the south and east sides of the tower completed its isolation from the rest of the building.

To the south of the tower a block of four or five rooms was probably once covered over, and the most interesting of them is certainly a long rectangular chamber, which may once have been a place of prayer. Unfortunately there was no furniture left in the ruins of the lower storey to tell the tale, apart from the remains of a large reed mat, some seven or eight feet wide, at the southern end of the room. However, above the collapsed ceiling, the remains told a different story. The excavators found a broken structure, having a brick base covered with carefully shaped and smoothed plaster. The pieces were carefully wrapped in cheese cloth, pasted on the outside to give them some rigidity, and transported to the Museum in Jerusalem. There they were patiently reconstructed and found to constitute a narrow table, some seventeen feet long and twenty inches high, and one or two other tables rather shorter in length (pl. 22). These structures were associated with plaster benches which ran round the walls. Also reconstructed was a desk-top, divided by a ridge longitudinally into two sections, each with a small basin hollowed out at the top (pl. 23a). Two inkwells, one of bronze, the other of baked clay, and both containing remains of a carbon ink of the type used on the scrolls (pl. 23b), completed the picture. The archaeologists had discovered the very room where many of the Dead Sea scrolls had been written. The inkwells were of a Roman type, examples of which have been found in Egypt and Italy, and are of the 'non-spill' kind still to be seen in our schools in Britain. It seems probable that the bowls in the desk top were used to carry a purifying water into which the hands of the pious scribe would be dipped before commencing work on the Holy Scripture, or perhaps before writing the Divine Name.

To the east of the tower was a complex of rooms with a number of hearths which might well have been the communal kitchen, and later excavations brought to light a large dining-hall, with a pantry attached, containing over a thousand small dishes, neatly stacked in piles on the floor against the walls. The SE. corner of the building was occupied by the two cracked cisterns already mentioned, and, by them, a workshop with the remains of iron tools, and to the north, a latrine made on the well-proved septic tank principles. Surrounded by paving, a collar of pottery gave into a large bell of crude clay which was embedded into stones down to the marly layer of the terrace, making a small septic tank. There is also nearby a wash place with a large sink, to complete the toilet facilities of the Settlement.

As well as the Scriptorium, other rooms were found with plaster benches round the walls, all pointing to communal use, either for worship or for the council meetings mentioned in the Qumran literature.

The most striking characteristic of the monastery is the number and size of the water cisterns, and the complexity of the conduit systems. The earthquake ruined some, and when, on re-occupation, more were built, the water had to be diverted along new channels. But the maze became so complicated as changes were instituted to satisfy some new need or the pet scheme of an Overseer, that to sort them out has been one of the main difficulties of an already intricate excavation. The water system alone has probably accounted for a reduction of at least a centimetre in Father De Vaux's patriarchal beard, which he is apt to chew in moments of mental stress. On the western side of the monastery the remains of an aqueduct can be seen running back into the cliffs. If the visitor follows this double line of stones and climbs up some distance to the head of the Wady Qumran, he will come across a tunnel which has been cut out of the rock for several yards. He can crawl through without difficulty until he emerges at the source of the Settlement's water supply, two small dams built into the cliffs to catch any water that might course down the upper reaches of the Wady from the Judaean hills.

The cisterns in the Khirbet are well made and carefully plastered, with steps at one end leading down into the water, a characteristic and very necessary feature of Roman cisterns in the area, allowing of the drawing of water from whatever level it may be. The water thus collected from the head of the Wady would have to last nine or ten months of the year, so that it is not surprising that so much was required for a community of perhaps some two hundred souls. Besides that necessary for the sustaining of life, water purification rites played a large part in their religious devotions, and at least two of the cisterns are of a size and shape consistent with their use as baptisteries.

The Combing of the Cliffs

As was mentioned in Chapter 2, an expedition was launched in the spring of 1952 to search the cliffs behind the Settlement for a distance of five miles, its centre being the Khirbet. It was a joint venture again, this time of Father De Vaux and his team from the French School, and Dr W. Reed with a party from the American School. Between 10 and 29 March the party of seven archaeologists, each in charge of a gang of three or four Bedouin, explored hundreds of nooks and crannies in the hills behind the Settlement. Just what that involves can only be fully appreciated by a visit to the spot, but perhaps the plates of the area (16a, 17) might give some idea. The limestone of the crags lends itself particularly easily to fissures and clefts which could make ideal hiding places. No less than two hundred and thirty unfruitful soundings were made, and many of them perched high in the cliff sides, taking hours of stiff climbing to reach, let alone excavate. Thirty-seven caves or holes in the rock were found to contain pottery or other remains of human habitation, and twenty-five of these held pottery identical with that found in the First Cave and the Settlement, thus proving beyond doubt that they were used by the same people at the same time.

The sizes and general shape of the caves varied a great deal. Some were large and open and, having been used by shepherds over the centuries, were consequently archaeologically poor. Others were low and narrow, or mere cracks in the rocks, so that, although pottery and the like was found in them, it is doubtful whether they were ever used for habitation, but probably only for storage. It was not therefore surprising to find that a great many sherds from characteristic Qumran storage jars were found there, along with articles of day-to-day use like cooking-pots, juglets, bowls, and lamps. It appears, then, that the Sectarians had lived outside many of these caves, using them only for storage, whilst they themselves dwelt in huts or tents. Indeed, in one crevice, along with the usual hoard of pottery, were found several forked sticks, almost certainly tent poles. That they belonged to the same period as the pottery was certain, since the entrance to the crevice had been blocked in antiquity with heavy stones.

One significant negative feature of the search was the complete absence of money in the caves. This seemed to De Vaux to point to a communistic mode of living, where all financial transactions were carried out by the central authority of the Sect, and all wealth put into a common pool. As we shall see, the documents confirm this view, and make this surrender of all personal wealth a necessary condition of full membership of the Community.

The most exciting discovery of the expedition occurred on 14 March when the only scroll cave, later numbered Three, was discovered. It is some way north of the First Cave and near the limit of the explored area. The roof had fallen in long ago, with the result that very few parchment fragments were found, though the remains of forty jars and twenty-six lids testified to the possibility of there having once been a large library stored in the 'cave. Any disappointment on that account, however, was amply outweighed by the discovery near the entrance of two rolled-up strips of oxidized copper. They had originally formed one long strip, about 8 feet long and 11 inches wide, and the indentations of an engraved message could be vaguely seen from the outside surface. To my mind this is one of the most interesting of the Dead Sea scrolls, but its opening presented a number of problems which were not overcome until the whole document was cut into strips three years later in the laboratories of the College of Science and Technology in Manchester, England (pls. 14, 15, and Appendix III).

CHAPTER SIX

THE ORIGIN OF THE SECT

WE saw from the last chapter that the archaeological evidence provides a historical framework for the Qumran Sect, with a beginning in or soon after the reign of John Hyrcanus (135–104 B.C.), and a violent end shortly before the destruction of Jerusalem in A.D. 70. Within that framework we are now able to fill out the story with more detail, thanks to our historical sources and internal documentary evidence. Of most importance from this point of view are certain biblical commentaries found in the Qumran library. But it should be understood that these commentaries are very different from the objective expositions of biblical books which we find on our library shelves today. In the first place, the Qumran commentator is not at all interested in the historical and social context of the biblical prophecy. For him, every word of Scripture was pregnant with meaning for his own day, and it is in its contemporary relevance that the interpreter is interested. In the process of arriving at its import for his time, nothing is barred to the commentator: any twisting of the meanings of words, reference to variant traditions known to the author although not included in the text before him, word plays, and even rewriting the passage to suit his interpretation, all is legitimate to the Qumran writer who is himself fired with the spirit of prophecy. This 'eschatological knowledge', by which the signs of the times could be interpreted in the light of ancient prophecy, was a special divine gift, possessed by the Qumran writers as by Jesus and Paul, and indeed the light thrown by these Qumran commentaries on the treatment by New Testament writers of Scripture texts is worth looking at in a later chapter. But to us, seeking first-hand knowledge of the history of the Sect, these references by Qumran authors to contem-

porary events, in which they saw the signs of the coming of
the end of the age, and the new era, can, carefully treated,
be most valuable. I say carefully treated, for our authors,
as one suspects with certain New Testament writers, are
not above changing the events to suit the prophecy, as
well as the words of prophecy to suit the events. Furthermore, a convention of the Sect is generally to use biblical
pseudonyms in place of proper names in their religious
documents. Thus the Roman forces, whose unassailable
might made such an impression on their countrymen when
they swept through the country in the first century B.C.,
were referred to as the *Kittîm*, a word originally applied
in the Bible to the inhabitants of Cyprus. The Sect's own
leader was called the *Teacher of Righteousness*, or the *Righteous
Teacher*. Themselves they called the *Sons of Zadok*, thinking
doubtless of Ezekiel xl.46, or the *Children of Light* in con-
tradistinction to their religious opponents, the *Children of
Darkness*.

The Community believed, as presumably the Teacher
had himself said, that their leader had received a special
commission from God to gather certain of the Jerusalem
priests together and take them into the desert, as a closely
knit community of the faithful, there to remain, pure and
undefiled, during the present period of apostasy until the
end of the age and the coming of the Kingdom of God.
Then he and his band would form the nucleus of the new
Israel, and the millennium would have dawned for all
mankind. There is no doubt that the spirit of unity which
shines through the writings of the Sect, and the strictness
of their self-imposed discipline, points to the early influence
of a very strong personality, whose death, once the Sect
was formed, could not affect the basic order and firm
expectations and doctrines of the Community.

There are several references to the persecution of the
Teacher at the hands of another oft-recurring figure, the
Wicked Priest. He is the arch-villain of the drama, and to him
is referred any wicked person spoken of in biblical prophecy.
In a particularly important commentary on the book of

Nahum, it may be this person who is referred to under the pseudonym *The Lion of Wrath*, and, thanks to the added mention of certain recognizable historical events, it is not difficult to identify this figure with the Jewish priest-king, Alexander Jannaeus, who reigned from 103 to 76 B.C. Indeed, before the recovery of this commentary many scholars had noted how well this tyrant fitted the characteristics of the Sect's persecutor. From this and other references we can now draw up a tentative picture of the train of events leading up to the formation of the Sect and its exile to the desert.

It will be remembered that the Maccabean Revolt of 168 B.C., graphically described for us in the First Book of Maccabees, arose out of the determination of Antiochus Epiphanes, the Greek ruler, to impose a Hellenistic civilization on the culturally backward Jews. He was but following out the intentions of his predecessor, Alexander the Great, whose dream was to create an empire, bound not so much by the power of the sword as by the coherence of a common culture. Although Antiochus had a measure of success in Judaea among a 'free-thinking' section of the priesthood, he found, to his disgust, that there was a hard core of obstinate priests and people who refused to abandon the faith of their forefathers and be 'westernized'. Severe punitive measures merely brought the matter to a head, and, in the inevitable revolt which followed, the Jewish rebels won a series of brilliant victories under the leadership of the Maccabean family. In 165 B.C., they were able to rededicate a cleansed Temple in Jerusalem, and throw out the heathen altar with which Antiochus had most horribly defiled the Temple three years previously. There was naturally much rejoicing, and, indeed, the event is celebrated by Jewry to this day, but not all sections of the people were so pleased. Besides those who hankered after the new culture, there was still a hard core of orthodox Jews, led by a section of the priesthood, who saw the Maccabean victories at the best as 'a little help', as the book of Daniel calls them, a slight palliative for a sickness which went much deeper than mere victories on the field of battle could hope to assuage. For these people, the persecutions of Antiochus were merely just punishment meted out by God to His people for their neglect of His Law, and the breaking of His divine Covenant, made centuries before with Moses. What God required from the Jews was not the shattering of a foreign yoke, but the breaking of their own hearts in true repentance; not the building of a political kingdom under a war leader, but the formation of a theocratic community, ruled by a pious and God-fearing priest, a spiritual shepherd of his people. Many of these pious folk had fled before 168, believing it better to die of starvation in the desert than to deny their God amidst the flesh-pots of Jerusalem. When pursued by their enemies, they had submitted to death in their hundreds rather than take up arms to defend themselves on the Sabbath. The Maccabees had seen, however, that this was no way to fight a war, and had persuaded some, at least, to abandon their principles for the time being and sacrifice all to the immediate end of winning their political independence. But not all were so tempted, and many remained true to their Law, earning the name of the Pious Ones, or *Hasidim*. Out of this group we can almost certainly trace the origins of the *Essenes* and the *Pharisees*.

The doubts of the Hasidim were soon justified by events. The Maccabean House, or Hasmoneans, were awarded the High Priesthood of Israel, although their claim to this high office was, to say the least, tenuous. This was no mere religious archbishopric, but a divine office given by God to a priest of His choosing, by which he might in all matters govern the Chosen People. He was the spiritual and temporal head of the nation, supreme arbiter in matters of faith and conduct, and must himself fulfil certain stringent conditions of race and purity before he could take office. In the days of the hated Antiochus, the position had been thrown open to the highest bidder, following on the banishment of the pious Onias III, but it was little better now to hand it over into the bloody hands of a warrior chieftain.

Taking the fullest advantage of the weakness of their

Seleucid foes, the Hasmonean House greatly expanded the territory of their Jewish kingdom, and then took to themselves the title of King as well as High Priest. This was another step in the rising consternation of the orthodox priests and their followers, and matters reached a head one day during the Feast of Tabernacles, when they beheld the most hated of all these warrior priest-kings, Alexander Jannaeus, offering the holy sacrifice at the Temple altar. Not only were his hands stained with the blood of countless battles, but they believed he had no right to his high office since he was but the son of a slave woman, and thus not of pure descent. We are told that the people screamed abuse at him, and began throwing the citron fruits they carried as part of the celebrations. Jannaeus was not the man to take this lightly, and he set his mercenary troops on to his own people, massacring several thousands. Perhaps we should see the hand of the Scrolls Sect behind these events, for one of their documents looks forward to the time when 'bastards and sons of strangers' should never again set foot in the restored Temple of the New Jerusalem. In any case, it seems most probable that at this time the Teacher gathered together some of the faithful priests of the Holy City and fled to the deserts of Qumran. There they began their exile from mankind, which would end only when God saw fit to vindicate His faithful and bring in His Kingdom.

Following the massacre in Jerusalem, Jannaeus went off to fight more wars with his neighbours, and was heavily defeated by the Nabatean king, Obedas. He barely escaped with his life, and just managed to struggle back to Jerusalem, only to find that the Pharisees had taken this opportunity offered by his weakness to make open rebellion against him. After six years of civil war, they took the unwise step of seeking foreign aid, in the person of the Greek monarch, Demetrius III, Eucaerus. He arrived with an army and met the malcontents at Shechem, and together they dealt Alexander a crushing blow. But then Josephus tells us that strangely enough many of the rebels changed sides and joined Jannaeus' defeated army. Light on this event is, however, cast by the Qumran commentary on Nahum, which tells us that Demetrius had 'tried to enter Jerusalem'. This, of course, was the natural step for a victorious commander to have taken, but whilst it was one thing having a foreigner fight one's battles, it was another having him tread the sacred courts of the Holy City itself. So many of his supporters deserted him, choosing the lesser of two evils, that Demetrius was obliged to retire to Damascus. Alexander then set about rounding up those who had remained with his enemies, and, dragging them forth from their places of refuge, turned them over to his mercenaries to be crucified. We are told that the stakes were erected on the terrace below the palace, so that Jannaeus could enjoy the spectacle whilst carousing with his harem. He also commanded that the wives and children of the wretched victims should be massacred before their dying eyes.

This practice of crucifying his political enemies is credited to the Lion of Wrath in the Nahum Commentary, and it further comments that this was never before done in Israel, being essentially a foreign punishment. This studied reference to crucifixion in their writings might imply that they themselves were affected by this aspect of the Lion's brutality, and would find an explanation if some of their own number had been put to death in this way, the recognized punishment of rebels.

It is tempting to push our dramatic reconstruction further and see in this incident an allusion to the fate of the Teacher himself. But it must be confessed that his death is referred to only once explicitly in the scrolls, and then under the euphemism of being 'gathered in'. Nevertheless, a commentary on Habakkuk tells us that the Wicked Priest confronted the Teacher and his followers one Day of Atonement in 'the house of his exile', in order to 'swallow him up in the vexation of his wrath', which tautologous phrase I have suggested elsewhere may conceal the more cogent 'to make him swallow from the cup of his poison', again a common euphemism for violent death. Other evidence has led me to suggest that Khirbet Qumran was none other than the *Bethome* (also called *Bemeselis*) to which Josephus tells us the ringleaders of the revolt against Jannaeus fled, and from which they were dragged forth to be crucified in Jerusalem.

From the very meagre evidence at present available, then, we might picture the Scrolls Sect as being intimately connected with the beginnings of the revolt against Jannaeus, fleeing to the desert under the leadership of their Teacher, and subsequently offering sanctuary to their erstwhile comrades when the revolt finally failed, and perhaps suffering with them the terrible fate ordained by the hated priest-king in Jerusalem.

However, with greater or lesser evidence, other scholars have fastened upon almost every other known Jewish High Priest of the Hasmonean dynasty for the title role of Wicked Priest in the scrolls drama. Again, largely as a result of disturbing comparisons that have been made between the Qumran Master and Jesus, almost all have hotly denied that the extant evidence allows of the martyrdom of the Teacher by crucifixion or any other means.

Unfortunately, it appears unlikely that we shall ever have a complete picture of the Teacher's life and death to satisfy our historical inquisitiveness, for such connected narratives have no place in Qumran literature. We should be wise at this stage to avoid too dogmatic assertions about the life of the Teacher or the manner of his death, or make too sweeping comparisons or contrasts with the Christian Master of whose own history, after all, all too little has come down to us that can be taken as incontrovertible fact.

CHAPTER SEVEN

THE LIFE AND DISCIPLINE
OF THE SECT

FOR our information about the rules of initiation and conduct of the Sect we are mainly dependent on the *Damascus Document*, so-called because it describes the place of exile of the Sect figuratively as 'Damascus' after Amos v. 27, and, probably, Zechariah ix. 1, and an almost complete work found in the Qumran library called *The Rule of the Community*, or more popularly nowadays, since its translation by the American scholars, *The Manual of Discipline*. This last work had also two appendixes, the *Rule for all the Congregation of Israel in the Last Days* and a collection of *Benedictions*. Both the *Manual* and the *Damascus Document* talk of another handbook which had to be known perfectly by the leaders of the Sect and taught to the younger members, called the Book of Hagī (or Meditation). So far no identifiable remains of this work have appeared, but it is possible that we have it without knowing, since, apart from possible quotations in the *Manual* and the *Damascus Document*, the book is quite unknown.

The Sect knew itself primarily as the 'Covenant' (*běrīth*), and specifically as the 'New Covenant' (*běrīth hǎdāshah*). Other names were the 'Congregation' ('*ēdah*), 'Assembly' (*qahal*), 'Party' ('*ēṣah*, sometimes also meaning 'Council'), and 'Community' (*yahad*), a word conveying the idea of 'unity', and these last two are often combined into 'Party of the Community' ('*ēṣath ha-yahad*). This idea of unity lay very close to the heart of the Sect, and the same word *yahad* is used very often adverbially meaning 'in common'. Thus they shared all the necessities of life, spiritual as well as material:

For everything shall be (held) in common, Truth and fair humility, and faithful love, and just consideration for one's fellow in the holy Council . . .

There was no place for the egoist in such a gathering:

No man shall walk in the stubbornness of his heart to err after his own will, eyes and purpose.

They took their meals communally, and sang their praises to God together, and in joint session held their deliberate councils. When one became a full member of the Sect, he 'mixed' his worldly possessions in the common pool, and he received back only the necessities of life. However, it should not be thought that this was an egalitarian society, where each man was as good as his fellow. We have frequent mention of their 'ranks', and according to their respective status in the society was their order of seating in the deliberative assemblies, of their speaking, and in fact of practically every communal activity. And in everything the priests had precedence. It is true that in a special sense the whole Community saw themselves as a joint priesthood,

an eternal planting, a holy house of Israel, an assembly of supreme holiness for Aaron . . .

but beginning as a priestly society, founded by a priestly Teacher, it was the priestly element which held the casting vote in matters of moment concerning the whole of the Community. In any group of ten persons, one had to be a priest, and the laymen had to sit before him according to their rank. Nevertheless, the government of the Community seems to have been run on democratic grounds in that, with certain safeguards, any member could speak, and all could vote. The priesthood formed a kind of Second Chamber, and their decision was regarded as divinely inspired, and was revealed by a 'casting of the lot', probably some oracular device such as the biblical Urim and Thummim.

The Sect thought of itself as the true Israel, and tried

to model its organization on the pattern of the ancient Israel of the Desert Wanderings. Thus they speak of 'camps' and divided themselves ideally into tribes, thousands, hundreds, fifties, and tens as in the book of Numbers. They had two main chiefs: a priestly 'Inspector' (*pāqîd*) and a 'Superintendent' or 'Overseer (*mebaqqēr*) of all the Camps'. The former's duties were mainly religious and included the spiritual examination of candidates for membership. The general Superintendent was responsible for matters of administration like work and finance, and there was similarly an Overseer in each 'camp' who combined with these executive duties the guidance and instruction of candidates for initiation. This curious combination of administrative and religious duties is found again in the *episkopos* or Bishop of the early Christian Church.

Among his duties the Overseer conducted the joint sessions of the Congregation, the ordering of which might well strike a fervent chord in the hearts of many committee chairmen today:

Every man (will be placed) according to his rank. First the priests will sit down, second the elders and then the remainder of all the people according to their respective ranks. In this order shall they be asked concerning a decision or any counsel or matter which shall concern the Many, and each man shall recount what he knows to the Council of the Community. Let no man interrupt his fellow whilst he is speaking, and let no man jump his assigned position to speak. The man who is asked to do so shall speak in his turn. And in a session of the Many, let no man say anything displeasing to the majority or which is not by direction of the Overseer. If any man who is not in the position of Interlocutor of the Many wishes to speak, let him rise to his feet and say, 'I have something to say to the Many'. If they call him, he shall speak.

It may be added that any infringement of this almost unbelievable good order was severely punished.

The executive head of the Party seems to have been a special Council of twelve men and three priests, ideally representing the twelve tribes of Israel and the three priestly families descended through the three sons of Levi.

There were also panels of judges, twelve in number according to one document from Cave Four, and ten in the *Damascus Document*, consisting in this case of four priests and six laymen, all of whom must be well versed in the Book of Meditation and the Law of Moses, and none younger than twenty-five or older than sixty.

Here is a summary of the penal code as given in the *Manual*. Exclusion from the 'Purity of the Many' means a temporary or permanent excommunication from full initiation, so that the offender is reduced, as it were, to the ranks, being of no higher status than that of a probationer. 'Fining' means a deprivation of rations, serious enough in a Community which would in any case be living on the bare necessities of life.

For deliberate lying in the matter of personal possessions – exclusion from the Purity of the Many for one year, and one quarter rations.

Bearing a grudge unjustly against one's fellow – six months (a later hand has written above the line 'one year'), and taking personal vengeance – the same.

Foolish speech – three months.

Interrupting another person speaking – ten days.

Sleeping during a session of the Many – thirty days.

Leaving a session without permission or good reason, up to three times in a single session – ten days.

Unnecessary self-exposure – six months.

Indecent exposure during bodily movement – thirty days.

Spitting during a session of the Many – thirty days.

Foolish laughter – thirty days.

Slandering one's fellow – exclusion for one year; slandering the Many – banishment for ever.

Murmuring against the institution of the Community – banishment for ever; against one's fellow – six months.

A man who is so overawed by the institution of the Community as to betray the truth and walk obstinately alone, and yet he returns – two years. In the first he will not touch the Purity of the Many, and in the second he will not approach the Banquet of the Many but shall take his place after all the others. When his two years are completed, his case will be investigated and if they admit him, he will be enrolled according to his rank, and may therefore be consulted in judgement. A veteran of more than ten years, however, who shall similarly default, shall return no more, and anybody associating with such a person will suffer the same fate.

That women and children had some place in the Community is shown by the heading of the *Manual*:

when they come they will gather together all the arrivals, women and children, and will recite (in their ears) all the statutes of the Covenant.

Then, in discussing the upbringing of boys, it lays down that a lad may not take a woman to wife until he is twenty, by which time he should know the difference between good and evil. Then he must realize the responsibilities involved, for, from that time, the wife may witness against him in process of law and may take part in the deciding of the issue. More material evidence of the presence of women at Qumran has been the discovery of female skeletons in the cemetery. Furthermore, some of the rules of the *Damascus Document* seem to have been formulated with a view to family life and speak of orphans and unmarried women requiring help.

In the matter of divorce the Covenanters have a similar attitude to that attributed to Jesus in the so-called Sermon on the Mount (Matthew v. 31–2). Thus, against the rabbinic custom of allowing divorce freely, the *Damascus Document* condemns 'marrying two women during their lifetime'. Like Jesus, too, it quotes as support for this rule Genesis i. 27:

Male and female created He them.
(cp. Matthew xix. 4; Mark x. 6.)

Indeed, in the scrolls we have already Jesus' extension of the biblical law against adultery to the lustful glance that precedes the act itself (Matthew v. 27–8). Thus we read of 'lusting after the eyes', and of 'the stubbornness of a sinful heart and eyes of lust', to which may well be compared the words of Jesus:

Hardness of heart suffered you to put away your wives
(Matthew xix. 8).

All in all, it seems the Covenanters had none too high
an opinion of the fair sex, believing them all potential
seducers of men from the strait and narrow way. One
document from the Fourth Cave warns its readers against
the wiles of the harlot, although probably using the figure
to represent the dangerous philosophies of the pagan world:

Vain are the words of the harlot,
and [. . .] errors.
She is continually trying to sharpen her words,
mockingly smoothing the way,
    and bringing *men* into derision with her shallow sentiments.
Her heart's crookedness prepares the way for lechery,
    her emotions [. . .].
In perversion they handle her befouled organs of lust,
    they penetrate the orifice of her legs in wicked acts,
and behave with guilty rebelliousness.
    [. . .] pits of darkness,
the sins within her skirts are many;
    her garments are the murk of twilight,
her adornments are tainted with corruption.
    Her bed is a couch of defilement,
[. . .] depths of the Pit.
    Her lodgings are beds of gloom,
and her domain is the depths of the night.
    From the pits of Hell she takes her dwelling
and lives in the tents of the underworld
    in the midst of eternal fire
y*t has no part in shedding light.
    She is the foremost of the ways of sin
and alas! all who take her will come to ruin.
    Those who clutch her will be desolate,
for her ways are the ways of death,
    her paths are the highways to sin,
her tracks lead into byways of iniquity
    and her paths are the guilt of transgression.
Her gates are the gates of death,
    He stalks in the entrance of her house.
All who [. . .] will turn back to Hell,

All who take her will go down to the Pit.
She lies in wait in the secret places [. . .]
she displays herself in the city's broad streets.
In the town gates she takes up her position
and no one moves her on.
Her eyes glance keenly hither and thither
beneath her voluptuous heavy lids,
looking for a righteous man to seduce him,
a perfect man to make him stumble;
upright men to lead them astray,
those chosen for rectitude to shun the commandment;
to make fools of the virtuous with lust,
to lead men of character to break the law;
to make the humble rebel from God,
to turn their steps from the way of righteousness,
to guide men into the ways of the Pit,
and seduce by flattery the sons of men.

This apparent distrust of women may have been carried
by some sections of the Order to the point of avoiding
marriage altogether. In this we have one of the many
correspondences between the Scrolls Community and an
ancient Jewish sect known as the *Essenes*, described to us by
Josephus and other historians. We shall have occasion to
refer to them frequently, and most scholars believe that
the Covenanters of the Scrolls are to be identified with at
least one branch of the Essene movement. A section of the
Essenes were celibate, and it is interesting to find that one
of the Qumran documents seems to modify certain biblical
ordinances with just this kind of situation in mind. Thus,
although Exodus xxii. 16–17 requires a man seducing an
unbetrothed virgin to marry her and pay her father an
appropriate dowry (Deuteronomy xxii. 29 adding that he
should not thereafter be allowed to divorce her), the
Qumran document says that the offender should merely
be fined two minas (i.e. a hundred shekels, the fine required by Deuteronomy xxii. 19 from a husband falsely
accusing his newly-wed wife of unchastity) and be expelled
from the community for life. The passage actually runs:

If they defame a man concerning a virgin of Israel: if his taking her was by [. . .], let him say so, and they shall examine her as to her integrity; and if he has not lied about her, she shall be put to death. But if by [. . .] he humbled her, he shall be fined two minas and be expelled all his life.

The gaps in the fragmentary text at this point are particularly vexing: the second must have contained a word meaning 'force' or the like, so that the act of which the man stood accused would be rape. In this case his punishment seems, at first sight, rather lenient, for the Bible requires the death penalty for a similar offence against a betrothed maiden where the circumstances give her the benefit of any doubt about her acquiescence in the act (Deuteronomy xxii. 25). However, it must be appreciated that expulsion from the Community could be tantamount to a death sentence. The Sectarians were required by their oaths to observe strict dietary laws and were forbidden to share the food of outsiders. Josephus tells us that similar conditions were laid down for the Essenes, and that if they were expelled from their communities they were reduced to eating grass and eventually died of starvation.

The first lacuna in our text could be restored either with some word meaning 'consent', implying a very harsh attitude indeed towards the woman, or, more probably, I think, a word like 'witchcraft'. Exodus xxii. 18 follows the law on seduction immediately with a condemnation of the 'sorceress', a word which elsewhere in the Bible can have a special reference to sexual allurement.

In any case, the attitude to women implied by our scroll is, to say the least, critical and unflattering. As Josephus says of the non-marrying Essenes: 'They do not as a matter of principle condemn matrimony, but they want to guard themselves against the licentiousness of women, and are convinced that none of them remains faithful to one man.' Philo in his *Apologia pro Judaeis* quotes even more scathing opinions held by the Essenes on womankind generally: she is 'selfish, excessively jealous, skilful in perverting her husband's morals and seducing him by never-ending charms.'

The Essenes, according to our sources, dressed in the simplest of clothes. Each postulant is given a single white garment on his reception into the community, but since this, like their other possessions, was held in common, the practice could give rise to some difficulty. There is a biblical law that forbids the wearing by men of women's clothing and *vice versa* (Deuteronomy xxii. 5). Presumably this was originally intended to be a precaution against some forms of sexual perversion, but to the Covenanters it seemed that their practice of wearing garments that might be used by either sex could give rise to a breach in the Law. Thus we find a document in the Fourth Cave collection which defines the position more exactly:

Let not a man's garb be upon a woman. Every [...] may be covered with a woman's *śimlah* robe, but let him not wear a woman's *ketōneth* under-tunic.

In the Old Testament, a *śimlah* robe is the outer garment of both men and women, or it can be applied to clothing generally. The *ketōneth* is an undergarment, like that doffed by the Shulammite before retiring to her bed at night (Song of Solomon v. 3).

Whilst on the subject of kit issue to the Essene postulant, Josephus tells us that everyone was issued with a small mattock. When he wished to relieve himself, he dug a small hole in the ground, squatted in such a way that his robe afforded maximum privacy, and afterwards filled in the hole with his mattock. Just such an instrument has, in fact, been found in one of the Qumran caves!

It appears that the Essenes were scattered throughout Palestine, living in colonies attached to the towns and villages. Every travelling member of the Order could avail himself of the communal property of these colonies and need therefore carry no provisions with him. In like manner Jesus could send his followers around the country assured of the hospitality of sympathetic communities (Matthew

x. 10f., etc.), and our Covenanters also had rules for sustaining the passing traveller who was of their persuasion, that is in their parlance, 'of Israel':

If a man makes a threshing floor or a wine-press and there comes to it one 'of Israel' who is destitute, he may eat and gather for himself . . .

Incidentally, it may be thought that such a regulation seems singularly out of place in a monastic community which was trying to keep itself as far apart from the rest of mankind as possible. It is, in fact, only one of a number of regulations which seem to have more relevance to the kind of urban community of Essenes described for us by Josephus and others than to this particular ascetic group at Qumran. The historians allow in their descriptions of the Order for such a 'mother' community in the Dead Sea wilderness, and it is usual to identify this with the Qumran establishment. It does seem however that we should beware in this case of applying everything we read in the scrolls specifically to this group in the desert, and reckon with the fact that we have in the scrolls a collection which may include quite varying ideas on matters of discipline, language, and perhaps even theology.

Initiation

The *Manual* lays down three stages through which the initiate must pass. The first, of unspecified period, is a matter of becoming acquainted with the spirit and practices of the Sect and is preceded by an examination, by the Inspector, of his motives and general outlook. At the conclusion of this stage, the Many debate his case and may, if satisfied, admit him to the next stage, or alternatively, can reject him altogether. If promoted, he will then pass into the Party of the Community, but without touching the Purity of the Many. At the end of a further year, a general session of the Community will deliberate on his suitability for further promotion and if favourably inclined, may admit him to the last stage, which again will last one year. In this last stage he will hand over to the Overseer all his worldly wealth, and it will be marked to his credit but not yet 'mixed' in with the common pool. He is still excluded from the Messianic Banquet, but is now apparently admitted to the Purity of the Many. If, on his completion of this stage, he is adjudged fit to enter full membership, he is enrolled and assigned a rank amongst brethren. Now, and only now, may he take his share in the Community decisions, be asked for his counsel, and permitted to pool his possessions with the Sect's. He has now entered the Covenant before God,

to do all that He has commanded, and to remain constant in following Him even in the face of terror, fright, or ordeal which may face him during the dominion of Belial.

At the initiation ceremony the priests and the Levites pronounce their blessings, praising 'the God of deliverances and all His deeds of faithfulness', and all the members say 'Amen! Amen!' Then follows a recitation of the wondrous works of God, His compassionate works of grace towards Israel, whilst the Levites recount the rebelliousness of the people and their sin under the dominion of Belial. Then those entering the Covenant make a general confession:

We have been perverse [. . .], we have done wickedly, we and our forefathers before us, walking [. . .] truth. But [God] is righteous, [who has executed] His judgements upon us and upon our fathers; and His faithful mercies he has bestowed upon us from everlasting to everlasting.

Following this, the priests bless the 'men of God's lot, who walk perfecly in all His ways', and say:

May He bless thee with every good: may He keep thee from all evil, and illumine thy heart with the knowledge of life, and favour thee with eternal wisdom. And may He lift up the face of His sure mercies upon you to everlasting peace.

The Levites then take up their curses upon the men of Belial's party, condemn them to eternal fire, and proceed to

give a solemn warning to those who would enter this sacred
Covenant that, should they prove unfaithful to it,

their lot will be placed in the midst of the eternally accursed.

Again the new members respond with the two-fold Amen.
This, we may be sure, is the service for reception of new
members, but we actually meet it in the *Manual* as the
annual Covenant service, where the membership of each
initiate is renewed by this service of self-dedication every
year, 'all the days of the dominion of Belial', in the order of
priests, Levites, and then the people, according to their respective ranks. Thus the Community is kept constantly
aware of its blessings and responsibilities and the ever
present struggle between the ultimate rule or kingdom of
God and the temporary dominion of Belial.

This rite of initiation into the full membership of the
Community was probably accompanied by an initial
baptism ceremony. Whether or not they used the great
cisterns at the Qumran Settlement for this purpose is still
open to question, as has been said in Chapter Five. Certainly
this would accord with the injunction of the *Damascus
Document* that no man shall bathe in water of less depth than
that required to cover a person, but whether this ruling had
relevance to baptismal ceremonies is not clear. It seems
more probable in some ways that the Sect would prefer the
traditional running water of the Jordan river not so far
away, or nearer still the clear waters of 'Ain Feshkha
– although at present these would only 'cover a man' if he
were lying down. We know very little about the actual
baptism ceremony, although some fragments from the
Fourth Cave tell us something about the benedictions used
at this rite. Once a person had been admitted to the Purity
of the Many he could be baptized in the same water as
other full members, but the Sect was careful that no novitiate
or non-member was allowed to touch this water, nor any
of his possessions, since he was ritually 'unclean':

Let him (the 'sinner') not enter the water to come into touch
with the purity of the holy men. For such shall not be cleansed

until they have repented of their wickedness; for uncleanness is on all transgressors of His word.

Salvation could come to the Qumran Covenanter only by complete separation of himself and his possessions from the world. This was not prompted by any smug self-righteousness on his part, but because he sincerely believed that pollution from the non-purified world meant the risk of contact with the dominion of Belial or the Devil, which might compromise the constant battle he was fighting within himself against the powers of evil. We shall have more to say on this matter when discussing the theology of the Sect, but the same idea prompted their strict disciplinary measures against any defaulting member on what might seem to us trivial faults. To the Sect, the slightest falling away from their very high standards of conduct and ritual purity meant that the member responsible had been brought into the power of the Devil, even though only for a fleeting moment of weakness, but yet in that time had proved himself a weak link in the chain of their defence against the dominion of Belial. Once let the powers of evil get a hold on a man, and he might prove a source of added temptation to other brethren, who must at all costs be protected in this critical time preceding the end of the present world order. Thus the initiate

will not unite himself with him in his work or his wealth lest he cause him to incur the guilt of transgression: for he must keep far from him in every matter . . . for all who are not reckoned in His Covenant are to be separated, they and all their possessions, and the holy man is not to rely on vain works, for vain are all those who know not His Covenant.

For this reason the rules for initiation are very exacting. This was no missionary Sect, going out into the world looking for members. People who desired the hard and pure life of the Covenanters with its promised blessings of the messianic age came to them and devoted themselves entirely to the cause, withholding nothing. If they came merely because they had suffered disappointments in life or had personal troubles or the like, the chances were that they would soon tire of the tremendous sacrifices demanded of the Sectarian, and fall by the wayside. Such people had to be rooted out before they came near the Purity of full members, hence the long and searching probation. One cannot doubt that at this stage many were turned away, and few reached the full initiation.

The Daily Life of The Covenanter

There is little in the literature so far recovered from Qumran which tells us much about the secular activities of the Covenanter, but a certain amount can be reconstructed from the excavations of the Khirbet. There were certainly the usual domestic tasks to perform, such as cleaning the communal rooms and kitchens, sweeping the plaster floors, raking over those of beaten earth. Some would work in the pottery workshops, preparing the clay, turning the vessels on the wheel, or firing the fashioned jars. The kitchen ovens have been found where the cooks prepared the communal meals, and the pantry where the simple crockery was stacked for the use of the Sectarians in the long dining-hall next door. Continual attention must have been given to building repairs and alterations, and in the winter the water conduits would need to be kept clear of mud and other blockages preventing the desperately needed supply to the cisterns. No doubt the repair of the aqueduct itself was an annual task round about October after eight or nine months of summer drought. At this time the empty cisterns would be examined for cracks in the plaster which, if not repaired in time, would allow the precious water to seep away into the ground. The simple reed and marl roofs would require attention after the summer's sun, if they were to withstand the heavy winter showers. And all through the year the shepherds and goatherds tended their flocks in the vicinity and particularly by the fresh vegetation of the 'Ain Feshkha, where doubtless simple farming also was carried on by the members to provide food for their Community.

From the Scriptorium would come the steady scratching

of pens, as the scribes copied their precious scrolls, and near by their fellows prepared the inks and skins for their use. Perhaps the women of the Community would be weaving the flaxen cloths for wrapping scrolls for storage, and either in the Settlement or in the caves a librarian was at his task of sorting and classifying the texts.

And all the time, day and night, came the chant of the recited Law or the hymns of thanksgiving. The duty of studying the Mosaic Law was taken very seriously. God's command to Joshua that

this book of the Law shall not depart out of thy mouth, but thou shalt meditate therein day and night ...

was carried out to the letter by the Community:

Let the Many keep awake in community a third of all the nights in the year in order to read aloud from the Book and to expound Judgement and to sing blessings altogether.

Here is one of the hymns they sang, as recovered from their scroll of Thanksgiving Psalms:

I thank thee, O Lord,
That thou hast tied my soul in the bundle of life
  and fenced me about from all the snares of the Pit.
Ruthless men have sought my life,
  because I hold fast to thy Covenant.
But they are an empty crowd, a tribe of Belial,
  failing to see that in thee is my foothold:
that thou, with thy mercy, wilt deliver my soul,
  for my footsteps are of thine ordering.

Even their striving against me comes from thee,
  that thou mayest be glorified in thy condemnation of the
    wicked,
and that thou mayest be magnified in me before men,
  for I stand by thy grace.
And I said, Warriors are encamped against me;
  they surround me with every warlike weapon,
and shower down arrows without relief.
  The spearhead flashes like a forest fire,
the din of their shouting roars like the flood,
  like a storm driving havoc before it ...

But as for me, when my heart dissolveth like water,
   then my soul takes strength from thy Covenant;
and the net they prepared to catch me
   will entangle their own feet;
and the traps they set for my soul,
   will cause their downfall.

And out of their midst I will bless thy name.

The following are extracts from other hymns of the collection, chosen mainly from the point of view of their theological interest.

   I thank thee, O Lord,
that thou hast redeemed my soul from the Pit
   and hast raised me from Hell's Abaddon to the Everlasting
      Height.
And I shall walk in the boundless plains,
   and know that there will be a final gathering
for those whom thou hast created from clay
   to join an eternal Council.
Thou hast purified the perverted from the great transgression
   to stand alongside the army of saints,
and to enter the throng of the angels of heaven.
   And thou hast allotted to men an everlasting
     portion with the spirits of knowledge,
to praise thy name in the Community,
   and to recount thy wonders before all thy Creation ...

   And I am dust and ashes;
What shall I purpose without thy good pleasure,
   and what shall I devise without thy good will?
How shall I be strong unless thou supportest me,
   and how shall I have wisdom unless thou createst
     it for me?
And how shall I speak but thou dost open my mouth,
   and how shall I answer but thou dost give me wisdom?

   Behold, thou art the prince of gods ('ēlīm),
King of the glorious ones, and Lord of every spirit,
   Ruler of all Creation, and apart from thee
     nothing was made.
Nothing is known without thy good will, and there is none
     save thee.

There is none beside thee in strength,
and none before thee in glory,
   and to thy greatness there is no price . . .

I thank thee, O Lord,
That thou hast made me wise in thy faith,
   and hast given me knowledge in thy wondrous mysteries,
in thy faithful mercies to [. . .] man,
   in thy many compassions to the perverse of heart.

Who is like thee among the gods, O Lord;
and who can match thy fidelity?
   Who can be justified before thee in his judgement?
No spirit shall argue with thy reproof,
   and none shall stand before thee in thine anger.
But all thy faithful children
   shalt thou bring in forgiveness before thee,
[cleans]ing them from their iniquities by thy great goodness,
   and by the abundance of thy mercies
thou dost cause them to stand before thee,
     for ever and ever.

For an everlasting God art thou,
And all thy ways are established for eternity
   and there is none beside thee . . .

During the night, as some slept in their tents and huts under the cliffs round about, and their brethren in the Settlement kept up this continual chant of hymns and readings, some of the elders would be standing in the watchtower, gazing at the skies, noting the movements of the moon and stars. We have a number of their works referring to the movements of the heavenly bodies, and not all their study was of purely academic interest. For them the stars and their positions could affect men's lives, and amongst their esoteric documents we have one giving the signs of the Zodiac distributed over the days of the month. Natural phenomena occurring at those times could be used to predict certain events. Thus:

if it thunders in the sign of the Twins – terror and distress caused by foreigners . . .

Another such astrological work, written this time in a secret code of their own devising, portrays the influence of the heavenly bodies on the physical and spiritual characteristics of those born in certain sections of the Zodiac. Thus, for example, a person born under Taurus, the Bull, will have long and lean thighs, narrow toes, and a humble demeanour. He will have inherited a balance of good spirit against bad, in the proportion of six to three. On the other hand, a rascal cursed with a proportion of eight parts of bad spirit to only one of good may be expected to display a somewhat coarse appearance with broad, hairy thighs and short, stubby toes and fingers.

The general rule seems to be that the better endowed a man is spiritually, the more ascetic his appearance. Thus in direct opposition to the last example, the saint-like person who has inherited no less than eight parts from the 'House of Light', as the scroll puts it, and but one from the 'Pit of Darkness' will rejoice in 'eyes that are black and glowing', will have a curly beard, subdued speech, and fine and well-ordered teeth. He will be of moderate build, 'neither too tall nor too short', with smooth thighs and fine and tapering fingers.

This document is unfortunately only fragmentary and we lack information on the particular constellation that would herald the birth of one whose spiritual inheritance would come entirely from the 'House of Light'. He, surely, would be the Prince of Light himself, one of the titles given in the scrolls to the Messiah or Christ. Doubtless the Qumran astronomers would be searching the skies particularly for this conjunction of the planets, and we need not look far from Bethlehem to find a school of thought from which the Magi story of Matthew could have come.

The Qumran scrolls reserve their bitterest denunciations, as did John the Baptist and Jesus, for the spiritual leaders in Jerusalem. In their eyes the orthodox priesthood had betrayed the flocks committed to their care, leading them into false ways and defiling the Temple and its rituals with unlawful practices. Thus a Qumran commentator on the book of Nahum quotes iii. 4 and explains:

> Its interpretation concerns those who lead Ephraim astray, who, by their false teaching and their lying tongue and lip of deceit, lead many astray, kings, princes, priests, and people together with the resident alien. Cities and families will perish through their counsel, nobles and rulers will fall because of what they say.

Originally, as we have seen, it was the officiating of a spurious High Priest which had made the Temple sacrifices of no account, but in the Qumran documents we can also see another major point of difference between the Sect and the Jerusalem priesthood and cult. At Qumran, the Community was observing a different calendar from that in use in Jerusalem. Thus, in their eyes, all the Temple ritual there was being observed on the wrong days of the year and its efficacy thus hopelessly impaired. Something of the Calendar controversy reaches us from pseudepigraphal literature which, as we shall see, is closely connected with, if not emanating from, our Sect. Thus in the Books of the Heavenly Luminaries in Enoch, we have instructions vouchsafed by Enoch to Methusaleh, his son, as revealed to him by the angel Uriel. For the author, the year is composed of twelve months of thirty days each, with one day intercalated for each of the seasons, making 364 in all, and exactly fifty-two weeks. Thus the festivals will recur on exactly the same day each week of the year, as ordained 'in the heavenly tablets'. This again is the main preoccupation of the book of Jubilees, a work which purports to give the chronology of the principal events in Israel's history to the very day of the week. This work was a great favourite of the Sect, as we know from the ten fragmentary copies recovered from the Fourth Cave, and it is quoted in the *Damascus Document*, which says:

> And the statement of the epochs of Israel's blindness to all these may be learnt in the Book of the Divisions of the Times into their jubilees and weeks.

Plate 13a. Joins in a Fourth Cave document. The tears are ancient.

Plate 13b. Part of a Fourth Cave document showing clear signs of mutilation in antiquity with a knife or sword.

Plate 14. The copper scroll being cut open in a laboratory in Manchester.

Plate 15. A cut segment of the copper scroll.

Plate 16a. A view across the Qumran monaste[ ]
looking south. On the left is the Scriptoriu[ ]
with the Council Chamber adjoining to [ ]
west.

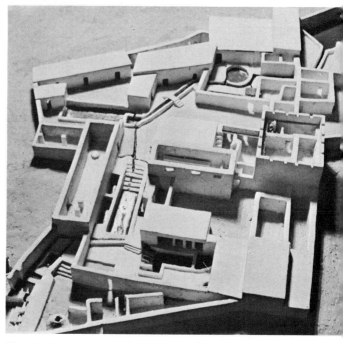

Plate 16b. A model of the Qumran monastery, looking westwards, as it may have looked about the time of Jesus, prepared according to plans published by the archaeologists.

Plate 17. The Hall of Congregation and Refectory of the Qumran monastery.

Plate 18. The large pottery kiln of the monastery at Qumran.

Plate 19. The cemetery of the monastery.

Plate 20. A water conduit feeding the great cisterns of the monastery.

Plate 21. The steps of a monastery cistern, cracked probably by the earthquake of 31 B.C.

Plate 22. The reconstructed writing tables from the Qumran Scriptorium.

Plate 23a (top right). Writing tables from the Scriptorium.

Plate 23b (bottom right). Inkwells from the Scriptorium, in terracotta and bronze.

Plate 24. Ancient Jewish tombs at the foot of the Mount of Olives.

And Enoch similarly points to the defection of men in not recognizing this ideal division of the periods:

in this men have gone astray, and are accordingly not to be numbered among the righteous.

The difficulty with this ideal calendar, of course, is that it does not fit the natural phenomena. As every schoolboy knows, the year consists of 365 and a quarter days, not of 364, and over a long period of years the difference is quite considerable. It seems probable that the error was rectified by the intercalation of a 'jubilee year', not a full calendar year but an interval after the end of each 'jubilee' of forty-nine years so that the Calendar could catch up on the solar cycle. The *Manual* has a section on the seasons which speaks of

the seasons of the years to their weeks (of years), at the beginning of their weeks to a season of liberation,

the last phrase presumably meaning this jubilee period of intercalation. Furthermore, scholars have recently shown that this old Jubilees calendar has a history going right back to the Exile, being used probably by Ezekiel, the priestly redactor of the Pentateuch, and the Chronicler to whom we owe the books of Chronicles and Ezra-Nehemiah.

One of the most hated innovations of the Hellenistic movement was the introduction of the Greek lunar calendar, with the periodic insertion of an intercalary month. Naturally, as with the language, day-to-day intercourse would make some sort of standardization of the calendar absolutely essential, but the Sect and other conservative bodies of Judaism saw this as just one more step in the abandonment of the faith of their forefathers and fiercely resisted it. One is reminded of the protests made in certain quarters in our own country at the introduction of daylight saving. But this went deeper for people like our Covenanters, for, particularly since the Exile, a great deal of the personal religious faith of the Jew centred in the Temple cult and observance of the festivals. It was thus a matter of vital importance for his whole religious life that those rites should be performed on the correct, and thus most efficacious, days. To break tradition on this point was to nullify the whole Temple ritual.

Thanks to certain fragmentary documents from the Fourth Cave, it has been possible to reconstruct in some detail the Sect's calendar. Theré is a group of manuscripts which deal with the duty roster for priestly families in the Temple, presumably for actual use when the new order had come about and they could return to the Holy City. One document gives a list of feasts, together with the priestly family on duty at that time.

It will have been noticed that when the Wicked Priest attacked the Scrolls Community in their 'house of exile', it is specifically said in the biblical commentary recording the event that it took place on their Day of Atonement, a Friday, according to their calendar. The rascally priest had chosen this particular occasion for his attack, knowing that at this time his victims would be restricted in their movements by religious custom. For him and his fellows in Jerusalem the Atonement Festival would have fallen on some other day.

We know of one rite peculiar to Qumran which probably became the sacramental focus of their worship, just as basically the same act did for the Christian Church. This was the Messianic Banquet, which is described for us in some detail in the *Rule for all the Congregation*:

[This is (the order of) the ses]sion of men of repute, [who are called] to meet for the Council of the Community. When [God] begets the Messiah with them, there shall come [the Priest], head of all the Congregation of Israel, and all the priests, e[lders of the children of] Aaron, [invited] to the Meeting as men of repute. And they shall sit be[fore him, each] according to his rank, corresponding to his st[ation] in the camps and marches. And all the heads of the el[ders of the Congregation] shall sit before them, each man according to his rank. And [when] they are gathered at the communion ta[ble, or to drink] the new wi[ne], and the communion table is laid out, and the new wine [mixed] for drinking, [let no man stretch forth] his hand on the first of the bread or the [wine] before the Priest; for [he will bl]ess the first of the bread and win[e, and will stretch forth] his hand on the bread first.

And after[wards], the Messiah will str[etch forth] his hands upon the bread, [and then] all the Congregation of the Community [will give bles]sings, each [according to] his rank. And after this prescription shall they act for every ass[embly where] at least ten men are assembled.

The chief actors in the Qumran Sect's Messianic Banquet, then, are the two Messiahs, i.e., the High Priest and the lay or Davidic Messiah, of whom we shall speak later, the priests, the heads of the thousands of Israel, the elders, and the Congregation. This will be the pattern of the Banquet to be held for the Elect who survive the great purging of the world in the last days. The last sentence, however, makes it clear that it could be a frequently observed ceremony involving far fewer participants than the numbers of the true Israel in the apocalyptic ideal, and since elsewhere in the *Manual* we have reference to the customary blessing of the bread and wine before partaking of the daily meal, it seems probable that every communal repast was considered to some extent a rehearsal of the Messianic Banquet. On the other hand, there is some evidence for a periodic observance of this act which exceeds in scope and importance the day-to-day communal feeding. In a trench dug through an open space near the Monastery walls, the archaeologists found some fifty jars or pots containing the bones of joints of meat, which had been boiled or roasted and picked quite clean. The animals involved were sheep, goats, and a calf, and were clearly the remains of meals, and presumably sacred meals, since considerable care and expense had been spent on keeping the bones free from pollution. The cooking bowls, for instance, were in some cases still quite complete and perfectly usable. They obviously could not be the remains of the daily repasts, since the number of burials would have had to run into tens of thousands, and, in any case, it is hardly likely that the Sectarians would be luxuriating every day on meat. They could, however, be the remains of an annual sacred meal, and one thinks at once of the Passover, which is not without its messianic connexions in later Judaism. However, it must be admitted that so far we have recovered no definite evidence linking the Messianic Banquet with the Passover.

Another curious fact for the life of the Sect emerges from a study of the Jubilees calendar. One of the strict injunctions of that work is that the Feast of Weeks must fall in the middle of the third month, i.e. the fifteenth day. This raises a problem at once, since the Law demands that this Feast must occur fifty days after the offering of the first sheaf, which was 'on the morrow of the Sabbath' (Lev. xxiii. 15–16). In the Jubilees calendar of a thirty-day month, this means that the point of departure must be the twenty-sixth of the first month, Nisan. But a Sabbath on the twenty-fifth of the month is impossible to a Jubilees calendar if the first day of creation, and thus of the first week of the year, was a Sunday. Sundays would then be on the first, eighth, fifteenth, twenty-second, and twenty-ninth days of the first month. The only way the Jubilees injunction could be made to work in practice would be if the year began on a *Wednesday*, giving Saturdays on the fourth, eleventh, eighteenth, and twenty-fifth days of the first month. Now from Exodus xii. 6 we learn that the Passover began on the fifteenth day of the first month, which under this system would be a Wednesday, and in a 364-day year would always be on the same day. The offering of the sheaf, then, on the twenty-sixth day would occur on the morrow of the Sabbath which follows the week of unleavened bread of the Passover festival. Mademoiselle Jaubert has made a particular study of the subject, and her examination of the patriarchs' movements recorded in Jubilees shows that the day most carefully avoided in their time-table, and thus the Sabbath, was not the *seventh* day of the week but the *fourth*, showing clearly that the Jubilees calendar began the year on the fourth day of the week, Wednesday, on the principle that it was only on that day that the heavenly luminaries were created, and thus one could not properly speak of 'day and night' before that (Genesis i. 14–19).

This reverence for Wednesday as the first day of the week has some rather interesting parallels which may not be unconnected with our Sect. A Jew of the first half of the tenth century, by name Al Qirqisānī, mentions in his book a certain religious sect called the *Maghārīya,* or Cave Sect, because their books were found in a cave (*maghār*), and places them historically after the Pharisees and before the Christians, but does not give their ancient name. These same people also receive mention by two Muslim authors, Al Bīrūnī (d. 1048) and Shahrastānī (d. 1153) both of whom seem to have been dependent on a lost ninth-century work on the *History of Religions.* Al Bīrūnī says of the calendar of the Cave Sect that it was on the night between the third and the fourth days, i.e. Tuesday night, that they

counted the days and months, and the great cycle of feasts commenced then, for it was on the fourth day that God created the great luminaries. Similarly according to them, Passover commenced on Wednesday.

Al Qirqisānī was of the Jewish sect called the Karaites, and it is remarkable that Karaite writings of the ninth and tenth centuries begin to show many points of correspondence with the Qumran Sect, which we shall discuss when looking at similar correspondences elsewhere about this time. But, in connexion with the calendar, it is interesting to note that the thirteenth-century chronicle of Bar Hebraeus mentions certain disputes which arose in the ninth century at Tiberias, where the Karaites were being accused of profaning the Sabbath and solemnizing *Wednesday.*

CHAPTER EIGHT

OTHER WORKS FROM THE
QUMRAN LIBRARY

THE Sect possessed many books which were not finally included in the biblical Canon, and which appear in the Protestant Apocrypha or have been collected under the title of *Pseudepigrapha*. Thus fragments of the original Hebrew version of the book of Ecclesiasticus, or the Wisdom of Ben Sira, were found in one of the Qumran caves. Tobit also has appeared, one copy in Hebrew and the other in Aramaic. Previously known mainly in the Greek recension, this is the first time we have seen the book in its oldest Semitic form.

We have already noted that the book of Jubilees was a great favourite with the Sect and has appeared in ten different manuscripts, one of them being written on papyrus. Previously the only certainly known versions of this work were in Ethiopic and Latin, and it is exciting to see the book in its original tongue and to compare these translations which seem, on the whole, to have been quite faithful to their original. The book of Enoch was another staunch favourite of the Community, and has appeared in ten different manuscripts, all in Aramaic, but possessing a very complex relationship to the Greek and Ethiopic versions so far known. Some sections seem to be entirely missing from these versions, such as a letter from Enoch to Shamazya and his companions which appears in the Qumran collection. Other parts are missing from Qumran although represented in the later translations, whilst several sections, particularly the astronomical Part III, seem to have had a separate circulation, though not always in the precise form of the later translations.

One of the most important works of the *Pseudepigrapha*

is that called *The Testaments of the Twelve Patriarchs,* which purports to give the last words of the twelve Israelite patriarchs to their sons.

Some parts of this work have long been recognized as Christian in origin, although the nucleus of the work was as clearly Jewish. Just how far Christian interpolation extends through the complete work has been a matter of great contention amongst scholars, and naturally it was of supreme importance to have pre-Christian copies of any part of this work to estimate the probable original strata. Now from the Qumran library we are able to see some of the source material of the Testament of Levi in its original Aramaic, with a text far longer than that of the Greek version in the *Testaments*. The source material, this time in Hebrew, of another of the *Testaments* has also appeared, that of Naphtali.

The very important *Manual of Discipline,* found nearly complete in the First Cave, has appeared in ten different manuscripts represented by the fragments, and very significantly for the history of the Sect and their ideas, these versions show some differences which can be traced to the process of compilation and selection. The oldest of these manuscripts goes back probably to the very beginning of the Sect, so that the work has clearly had a long and involved history.

The *Damascus Document* has appeared in seven different manuscripts, one of which is on papyrus, and some of the fragments have sections missing from the medieval copies from which we have hitherto known the work (see Appendix I). Thus, for example, parts of the original beginning and end are now extant, and we have part of the final summing-up of the work in the words:

and this is the explanation of the ordinances which they shall carry out throughout the whole of the period of [...] concerning the interpretation of the Last Torah.

This last phrase is particularly important for understanding the attitude of the Sect towards their own sectarian documents, which carried over, as it were, the Mosaic Law until the time of the coming of the One who could make a final interpretation, the Last Law of all for the new age.

The Qumran sectarians longed for the day when the Messiahs would lead them back to a new and purified Jerusalem, where they could again fulfil all the demands of a sacrificial cultus. One fragmentary work which has appeared in a number of copies has been entitled *A Description of the Heavenly Jerusalem* and contains a detailed vision of the Holy City and its Temple, doubtless inspired by the last chapters of the book of Ezekiel.

A representative group of pseudo-prophetical literature has appeared, much of it previously quite unknown. Included in this are the remains of five or six copies of a composition which is clearly modelled on the style of our book of Jeremiah, rather like the apocryphal Jeremiah-Baruch literature already known, yet not textually identical with any portion of it.

From the First Cave came an almost complete work giving the order of battle for an apocalyptic war between what are called 'the Sons of Light' and 'the Sons of Darkness' and five fragmentary copies have been found in the Fourth Cave which help fill out some of the lacunae in the large scroll. The combatants are further detailed as the Jews of Levitic, Judahite, and Benjamite ancestry, and their opponents are the forces of Edom, Moab, Ammon, and Philistia on the one hand, and the 'Kittim' on the other. The army of the Children of Light is based on a general mobilization of the people between the ages of fifteen and thirty, the cavalry corps between thirty and forty-five, officers between forty and sixty, commanders between fifty and sixty. The formal and artificial nature of these 'Queen's Regulations' will be apparent from the first, and continues in laying down a sevenfold volley from the slingers which precedes seven throws from the javelin throwers, who in turn open the way for the attack of the phalanx. All the operations are directed by the priests, who sound off the trumpet-calls, 'Advance', 'Attack', 'Retreat', 'Reassembly', 'Pursuit', and 'Ambush'. Before the attack, the whole army gives a great shout

> to strike terror in the heart of the enemy.

The Head Priest accompanies the army into the field, and prayers precede and follow the battle. Further indications that this is a religious war are contained in the mottoes of the banners which precede the various sections into battle. Thus before the main body goes the slogan 'People of God' with the names of Israel and Aaron and the twelve tribes of Israel. Before the regiments goes the strange device,

> The Wrath of God will burn against Belial and against the Men whose Lot is with him until None Survives.

Company standards had

> From God comes the force of battle against all Wicked Flesh,

and platoons were preceded by

> The place of the Power of Evil Men shall cease through the might of God.

Each squad carried

> Joyful praises with the harp (be unto) God.

Besides these there were special banners for the various stages of the conflict, all of which were laid down, including the temporary reversal. Thus on entering the field,

> Truth of God, Righteousness of God, Glory of God, Judgement of God

was displayed above all. When the army closed with the enemy they were cheered and the foes overcome with

> The Right Hand of God, the Appointed Time of God, the Tumult of God, the Slain of God.

On retirement, the Children of Light carried with them

> The Adoration of God, the Greatness of God, the Praises of God, the Glory of God.

Even the trumpets had mottoes. For instance the ones used for signalling pursuit had on them the apposite message:

God smiteth all the Children of Darkness; let not His Anger subside until they are destroyed.

After an initial defeat, the apocalyptic victory is won, and the victorious army returns to camp, and

Joyfully sing the hymn of returning, and the next morning wash their clothes and cleanse themselves of the blood of the guilty corpses, and return to the site of their stand where they had drawn up their army before the dead of the enemy fell.

There they all bless God together, saying,

Blessed be the God of Israel who is faithful to His Covenant and the testimonies of salvation for the people redeemed by Him.

Mr Yadin, the head of a more recent Jewish army, who has edited this work for the Hebrew University, claims to be able to find in its basic strategy correspondences with the Roman army manuals of the day, whilst others have thought that, although it reflects a genuine method of war-fare, it might be more akin to the Maccabean practices. But the apocalyptic nature of the battle it describes is clear, and when one stands in the middle of the pathetic ruins of their humble Settlement buildings at Qumran, and powders the charred remains of their roofs between the fingers, the dream of their Final War against the powers of Darkness and the reality of their conflict with a more material enemy seem worlds apart.

CHAPTER NINE

THE DOCTRINES OF THE SECT

THE basic philosophical and religious conception of the Sect is contained in their doctrine of the Two Spirits. Briefly this implies that there are in the Universe two spirits, one of good and the other of evil, respectively symbolized as Light and Darkness. Both are under the same supreme rule of God who will eventually give the victory to Good, but only after a prolonged cosmic battle. The war of the Spirits is reflected on earth in the tensions within every man for good and evil, as the *Manual* says:

And He assigned to Man two Spirits in which he should walk until the time of His visitation. They are the spirits of Truth and Perversity: Truth born out of the spring of Light, Perversity from the well of Darkness. The dominion of all the children of righteousness is in the hands of the Prince of Light so that they walk in the ways of Light, whereas the government of the children of Perversity is in the hands of the Angel of Darkness, to walk in the ways of Darkness. The purpose of the Angel of Darkness is to lead all the children of righteousness astray, and all their sin, their iniquities, their guilt and their rebellious works are the result of his domination, in accordance with God's mysteries until His appointed time. And all their stripes and seasons of affliction are consequent upon the rule of his (Satan's) hostility.

Thus the whole cosmos is divided for the time being into two camps, and as Man is apportioned these two spirits so will he behave:

Until now the Spirits of Truth and Perversity struggle within the heart of Man, behaving with wisdom and folly. And according as a man inherits truth and righteousness, so will he hate Perversion, but in so far as his heritage is rather from the side of perversion and wickedness, so shall he loathe the Truth.

As we have seen, another document tells us that his

'inheriting' of these Spirits depends on the stars at his birth, and even that the proportions within a man can be numerically reckoned.

Here are the fruits of the Spirit of Truth as enumerated in the *Manual*:

To enlighten the heart of Man and to make straight before him all the ways of true righteousness, to make his heart fearful for the judgements of God; a humble spirit, an even temper, a freely compassionate nature, an eternal goodness, and understanding and insight and mighty wisdom which believes in all God's works, and a confident trust in His many mercies, and a spirit of knowledge in every ordered work, and zeal for righteous judgements, and a determined holiness with steadfast mind; loyal feelings towards all the children of Truth, and a radiant purity which loathes every impure idol; a humble bearing and a discretion regarding all the hidden things of Truth and secrets of Knowledge.

The reward to those who show these qualities in their lives is

healing and abundant peace, length of life and fruitful seed with everlasting blessings, and eternal joy in immortality, a crown of glory and a robe of majesty in eternal light.

To be contrasted with this sublime state is the lot of those led by the Spirit of Perversion. Among the fruits of their Spirit are greed, injustice, wickedness, falsehood, pride, deceit, hasty temper, jealousy, lechery, blasphemy, spiritual obtuseness, and obstinacy, and vile cunning. No wonder that the best he can expect in the 'Day of Visitation' is

many stripes from the Angels of Destruction, in the everlasting Pit, through the overwhelming God of Vengeance, in everlasting terror and perpetual disgrace, with the shame of extermination in the Fire of the dark regions. And all their times for all generations will be in grievous mourning and bitter misfortune, in the dark calamities until they are destroyed with no chance to escape.

Since the Spirits are apportioned at birth, this apparent determinism may seem to override the bounds of justice. If a man, by his stars, is given a balance of evil in his character it seems hardly fair to condemn him to such punishment for eternity. The argument will have a familiar ring in these days of popular psychology, but the Qumran Covenanter, at least, had his answer. For all men there was one way of salvation, depending on his own will and the mercy of God. If he would but apply himself to the study of God's Word in humility and pious devotion, God would answer by granting him a restored cleanliness, a sense of perfection.

For it is ... through the submission of his soul to the statutes of God that his flesh may be cleansed ('flesh' being here exactly the Pauline *sarx*, the debased moral nature of Man) ... He will order his steps in the perfect Way and in all the paths of God ... not transgressing a single one of His words.

Man must prepare himself by self-discipline, but the action of cleansing is entirely dependent on the will of God. Man has no claim to justification merely on the grounds of his good works; it is an act of divine grace, as much in the eyes of the Covenanter as of Paul.

As for me [says the psalmist at the end of the *Manual*], my justification belongs to God, and in His hand is the perfection of my way ... and from the fountain of His righteousness (springs) my justification, a light in my heart.

And again,

if I totter, the covenant love of God is my eternal salvation, and if I stumble in the crookedness of my flesh, my justification depends on the righteousness of God, which is eternal.

The word used here for 'justification' is *mishpaṭ*, which also means 'judgement'. Man's justification is the pronounced verdict of God, a legal 'clearing' which by no means implies sinlessness. Rather, Man's iniquity has been cleansed by the grace of God: he is restored into true sonship and, in the words of another passage of the *Manual*, 'estimated perfect'.

In all this, many of my Christian readers will have begun to feel the warmth of a familiar hearth. Here are the ideas of the New Covenant, the emphasis on justification by grace and a doctrine of perfection. We are indeed bordering

very closely on to Christian soil and must accordingly begin
to weave our threads of Qumran theology into the fabric
of the New Testament to understand fully the considerable
significance of the new material for the history of the
Church.

Let us first return to the basic doctrine of the Two
Spirits. This is one of the favourite themes of Judaeo-
Christian writings. Indeed, one section of the very early
Didache or 'Teaching of the Twelve Apostles', dealing with
'The Two Ways', could almost be a literal translation of
this part of the Qumran *Manual of Discipline*. In the New
Testament the richest source of comparison is certainly in
the writings of St John. In his first Epistle there is hardly a
paragraph which does not contain some reference to the
opposition of Light and Darkness, of Truth and Error (a
legitimate translation of '*āwôn*, 'perversion', at root, anything 'twisted').

God is Light, and in Him is no darkness at all. If we say that we
have fellowship with Him, and walk in darkness, we lie, and do not
the truth (a favourite Qumran phrase): but if we walk in the
Light, as He is in the Light, we have fellowship one with another
(i. 5–7).

The spirits of this world must be tested and proved according to their response to the central fact of creation, the
Messiahship of Jesus:

Beloved, believe not every spirit, but prove the spirits, whether
they are of God: because many false prophets are gone out into the
world ... Hereby know ye the Spirit of God: every spirit which
confesseth that Jesus Christ is come in the flesh is of God: and
every spirit which confesseth not Jesus is not of God (iv. 1–3).

Perhaps most familiar is the Prologue of the Gospel:

In him was life; and the life was the Light of men. And the Light
shineth in the darkness; and the darkness apprehendeth it not ...
There was the true Light, *even the Light* which lighteth every man
coming into the world (i. 4–5, 9).

It is a fact that the Qumran library has profoundly

affected the study of the Johannine writings and many long-held conceptions have had to be radically revised. No longer can John be regarded as the most Hellenistic of the Evangelists; his 'gnosticism' and the whole framework of his thought is seen now to spring directly from a Jewish sectarianism rooted in Palestinian soil, and his material recognized as founded in the earliest layers of Gospel traditions.

In 'the Light which lighteth every man' we have explicitly the idea of apportionment of the Spirit of Light to Man at birth, and perhaps the enigmatic phrase in iii. 34,

> for he giveth not the Spirit by measure

has reference to the numerical division of Qumran. To John, the apportionment of the Spirit of Light to Jesus was such that he became Light itself: 'I am the Light of the world', and he records that the promise to those about him who would believe on him and his mission was that they should become 'sons of Light', the exact terminology used by the Sect to describe themselves in the apocalyptic war with the 'sons of Darkness'. Jesus speaks of a 'second birth' when a Man would 'be born of the water and the Spirit', and we might recall the Qumran psalm which speaks of God purifying

> some of the sons of man to abolish the spirit of perversion from his flesh, and to cleanse him by His Holy Spirit from all wicked deeds, and sprinkle on him the Spirit of Truth as purifying water.

Just as the Qumran sectarians waited for the final vindication of the Spirit of Light at the Time of Visitation, so to John, in a different perspective,

> the darkness is passing away, and the true Light already shineth (I. ii. 8).

This opposition of Light and Darkness, Truth and Error, owes much to Iranian thought, but it did not develop into an absolute dualism at Qumran as it did there. Both good and bad spirits are subject to God, although, naturally enough here, as in John, we are coming perilously near to a dualism in the personification of the Spirit of Evil in the Angel of Darkness, or Belial for Qumran, and Satan, the Devil, the 'Prince of this world', 'murderer from the beginning', for John. Demon possession is a necessary corollary of this doctrine, and of course occurs time and time again in the gospel stories, particularly in the healing miracles. Jesus used his authority as one abundantly 'possessed' of the opposite Spirit, to cast out the powers of darkness in the mentally sick. Thus his enemies' assertion that he was the Devil himself was quite absurd:

and if Satan casteth out Satan, he is divided against himself ... But if I by the Spirit of God cast out devils, then is the kingdom of God come upon you (Matt. xii. 26-8).

If Jesus is demonstrating the power of the Spirit of Light in this way against the powers of Darkness, it can only mean that the cosmic battle is nearing its climax in the universe, and the 'rule' or 'kingdom' of God is being wonderfully demonstrated in the world. God has at last come to the aid of a divided mankind, in the person of His Messiah, or Prince of Light, who enters the house of Satan, 'the strong man', and despoils it. The moral issues of the world take on their true colours: no longer do the greys and half-whites plague man's decisions, but he is confronted with blacks and whites, and the choice is clear-cut:

He that is not with me is against me (Matt. xii. 30).

To be kept constantly in mind when reading Qumran literature, as also the New Testament, is the sense of impending doom which pervaded religious thought of this time, and which at intervals, has done so ever since. We have already seen that the Qumran sectarians went into the desert to prepare for the Day of Visitation, and from there they viewed the terrible events in their land and read them as the 'signs of the times'. Jesus, too, is aware of a special tension in the world, coming to a climax as he faced his death, in which the Spirits of Darkness would make their final bid for supremacy, but which would, in its victory, usher in the new age. This time of trial would be shared by all living in those days, for in every man the forces of evil would increase their struggle against the powers of Light and Truth as the end drew near. It was a time of Temptation (*peirasmos* of the New Testament), and Jesus' hope for his followers was that they should be spared this terrible conflict within their hearts which he himself was undergoing as representative of mankind.

'Pray that ye enter not into temptation' is the keynote of his last messages, and when the climax was drawing near, and the forces of Darkness drew themselves together for the supreme battle, he bade his disciples keep awake in the Garden: 'Watch and pray, that ye enter not into temptation.' His pattern of prayer again sounds this note of urgency, though over-repetition would seem to have blunted it for most of us. 'Thy kingdom come' is no vague hope for the morrow, but a cry of anguish from the bottom of a tortured soul for the end of the Age, a release from the spiritual battle which the new age of Light and goodness would bring.

'Lead us not into temptation but deliver us from evil' is the plea of a soul battling within itself as the powers of darkness begin to pit their strength against an awakened conscience.

The Mysteries

Now God, through the mysteries of His understanding and His glorious wisdom, has ordained a set period for Perversion, and in the time of His visitation He will destroy it for ever. Then shall the Truth of the universe shine forth for all time.

Thus speaks the *Manual of Discipline*; now listen to Paul in his letter to the Romans:

according to the revelation of the mystery which hath been kept in silence through times eternal, but now is manifested (xvi. 25–6).

And again to the Corinthians:

but we speak God's wisdom in a mystery, *even* the *wisdom* that hath been hidden, which God foreordained before the worlds unto our glory: which none of the rulers of this world knoweth: for had they known it, they would not have crucified the Lord of glory ... But unto us God revealed *it* through the Spirit: for the Spirit searcheth all things, yea, the deep things of God (I. ii. 7–10).

And speaking to the Ephesians:

... how that by revelation was made known unto me the mystery, as I wrote afore in a few words, whereby, when ye read, ye can perceive my understanding in the mystery of Christ; which in other generations was not made known unto the sons of men, as it hath now been revealed unto his holy apostles and prophets in the Spirit ...; unto me ... was this grace given, to preach unto the Gentiles the unsearchable riches of Christ: and to make all men see what is the dispensation of the mystery which from all ages hath been hid in God who created all things (iii. 3–9).

So possession of the Holy Spirit was to Paul a means of unlocking these divine 'mysteries'. The Teacher of Righteousness of the Qumran Community also had access to these secrets, as we learn from the commentary on Habakkuk:

to whom God made known all the secrets of the words of His servants, the prophets.

Like Paul, the Teacher had the responsibility of passing on these secrets to his followers now that the long awaited end-time had come. He is called in another Qumran commentary 'the Mediator of Knowledge' and he is probably the author of the hymn who styles himself 'Mediator of Knowledge in the wonderful mysteries'.

This special knowledge into the divine mysteries is not so much the result of intellectual exercise, as a heavenly revelation, the nature of which in the Dead Sea scrolls, as in Christianity, is almost entirely eschatological. Thus Matthew records that when Jesus was speaking about the Day of Judgement, he went on,

I thank thee, O Father, Lord of Heaven and Earth, that Thou didst hide these things from the wise and understanding, and didst reveal them unto babes ... All these things have been delivered unto me of my Father: and no one knoweth the Son save the Father; neither doth any know the Father save the Son, and he to whomsoever the Son willeth to reveal *Him* (xi. 25-7).

The *Manual of Discipline* says:

He will purge by His truth all the deeds of Men ... to give to the upright insight into the knowledge of the Most High and into the wisdom of the sons of Heaven, to give the perfect way of understanding.

'The Sons of Heaven' are the angels who sit in the divine council chamber, and who thus have pre-knowledge of the celestial plans of operation, from which will ultimately result the apocalyptic acts of 'works of God'. Thus the Spirit of Truth enlightens a man to

an understanding and insight and mighty wisdom which believes in all the works of God.

The first and most essential preliminary to these apocalyptic 'works of God' is a belief in His messenger. Thus in answer to the question of his followers

What must we do, that we may work the works of God?
Jesus replies

This is the work of God that ye believe on him whom He hath sent. (John vi. 28-9).

Similarly, the Qumran commentator on Habakkuk ascribes deliverance from 'the House of Judgement' to 'suffering and belief in the Righteousness'.

One aspect of the 'works of God' as far as Jesus himself was concerned was the exercise of his powers of healing (John ix. 3). It demonstrated that at last a light had come into the world that could dispel the powers of darkness, including those devils that made men physically sick (John ix. 5). The Essenes also practised the arts of healing, as Josephus tells us, having received from the ancients their knowledge of therapeutic herbs and minerals. One of the more likely explanations of their Greek name (*Essaeoi* or *Essēnoi*) is that it corresponds to the Aramaic '*āsayyā*', 'physicians, healers', reflected in the name given in Philo's *De Vita Contemplativa* to their Egyptian counterparts, the *Therapeutae*.

In one Qumran scroll, an Aramaic treatment of the book of Genesis, there is a reference to the practice of healing by laying-on of hands. Abram is asked to attend Pharaoh after his affliction at the hands of God, to 'lay his hands upon him that he may live'. All recourse to other healers at the court had failed, 'for the spirit scourged them all and they fled'. However, Abram records his success:

I prayed [for him] ... and I laid my hands on his [head], and the affliction left him and the evil [spirit] was driven out [...] and he lived.

One is reminded of the woman with an infirmity in Luke xiii. 11–13:

When Jesus saw her, he called her, and said to her, Woman, thou art loosed from thine infirmity. And he laid his hands upon her: and immediately she was made straight, and glorified God.

It should be borne in mind that the healing 'miracles' performed by Jesus and his disciples were not merely kindly acts motivated simply by a common humanity: they were intended as apocalyptic signs by which the world might know that the kingdom was at hand.

Seeking after 'signs of the times' is a characteristic feature of any eschatological religion, and a favourite diversion of certain evangelical Christian sects today. Their treatment, or as some would say, maltreatment of the Bible, quoting passages out of context to support their arguments for believing that modern events foreshadow the end of the world, can certainly claim ample precedent in the Qumran scrolls and the New Testament. In both groups of literature, writers believing themselves inspired with this special knowledge, delve into the words of Scripture to lay bare the secrets of the last times. Often enough they show as much regard for the real historic circumstances of the prophecy as the young men who wave tracts in our faces on the doorstep.

Just as the Qumran expositors dissect the recorded words of the prophet Habakkuk to seek there references to their Teacher living some five centuries later, so for intsance Matthew delights in producing Old Testament texts to support the messianic claims he makes for his Master. Too often he merely succeeds in the eyes of the critic in casting doubt on the historicity of the events he records. They savour too much of being merely projections of current expectations based on this prognosticatory use of Scripture.

The fact is that for the immediate follower of Jesus an 'objective' history of his life would have seemed as pointless as a similar record of the Teacher of Righteousness for the Qumran Community. To attempt to read 'connected history' into the expositions of the Qumran commentators is completely to misunderstand their purpose.

It is worth our while to turn aside for the moment to look more closely into this question of the Qumran and New Testament use of Scripture as a pointer to the solution of a number of problems connected with both.

CHAPTER TEN

THE USE OF SCRIPTURE TEXTS IN THE DEAD SEA SCROLLS AND THE NEW TESTAMENT

VERY briefly, the problem of New Testament citations of Scripture is this: certain writers, and particularly Matthew, cite Old Testament passages in a way at variance with every textual tradition which has come down to us. That they should often follow the LXX against the Hebrew is to be expected, since the LXX was the Bible of the early Church, and it is also understandable that some of the quotations should have been taken from the Hebrew Scriptures, especially among the Jewish-Christian writers. What is more puzzling is where they quote a version which is otherwise completely unknown. Here are some examples.

In Matthew ii. 6, the evangelist is showing how Christ's birth was foretold by the prophets of old as taking place in Bethlehem, and to prove his point he quotes:

And thou, Bethlehem, land of Judah, art in no wise least among the princes of Judah: for out of thee shall come forth a governor, which shall be a shepherd of my people Israel.

Now Micah v. 2 actually says:

But thou, Bethlehem Ephrathah, which art little to be among the families of Judah, out of thee shall one come forth unto me that is to be ruler in Israel.

LXX differs little and no support for Matthew can be found in the other versions. But he has changed the whole sentence structure, implying that Bethlehem is not the least, whereas the Hebrew says he is, adds the conjunction 'for' to give his rendering any sense, alters 'families' (or 'thousands') to 'princes', omits 'unto me' and elaborates 'Israel' with 'my people'. The modernizing of the geography, 'Ephrathah' to 'land of Judah' is the least of his variants.

We have seen something of how the idea of the 'mysteries' and divine 'knowledge' permeates New Testament writings. Matthew finds some support for this idea in explaining Jesus' use of parables by quoting Psalm lxxviii. 2 in the form:

I will open my mouth in parables; I will utter things hidden from the foundation of the world (xiii. 35).

This is how the Psalmist's Hebrew is usually rendered:

I will open my mouth in a parable; I will utter dark sayings of old; which we have heard and known, and our fathers have told us.

Again Matthew has no support from the versions.

Palm Sunday's events are justified by Matthew by a particularly interesting composite quotation:

Tell ye the daughter of Zion, Behold, thy King cometh unto thee, meek, and riding upon an ass, and upon a colt the foal of an ass (xxi. 5).

This is how the Hebrew of Zechariah ix. 9 may be read:

Rejoice greatly, O daughter of Zion; shout O daughter of Jerusalem: Behold thy King cometh unto thee; he is just, and having salvation; lowly and riding upon an ass, even upon a colt the foal of an ass.

In Isaiah lxii. 11 we find:

Say ye to the daughter of Zion, Behold, thy salvation cometh.

Clearly both quotations have been joined together, but its composite nature is not the only peculiarity of this use of Scripture by Matthew. In his rendering he has divided the parallel stichoi of the Hebrew verse to imply that there were two separate animals involved, an ass and a colt. Note that the English version renders the Hebrew

an ass, even upon a colt ...

to show, quite rightly, that the one is, in the Hebrew, merely a synonym of the other. Mark and Luke speak of only one animal, but Matthew's quotation leads him in verse 7 into the apparent absurdity of the disciples putting their garments on both animals. Certainly the Matthaean school cannot be accused of not knowing Hebrew properly, and it is probable that another tradition is showing through here, possibly pre-Christian in origin.

Now in these three examples quoted, and there are many such, one point is common to all, that Matthew's versions of the texts favour his interpretation of the events. Thus the 'ruler' of Micah ('governor' in Matthew) has been supplemented by the title of 'shepherd', a conception of the Davidic ideal ruler which we see already in II Samuel v. 2 and Ezekiel xxxiv. 23 from which both this and the addition, 'my people', have come. The loose 'families' has been crystallized into 'princes', and 'Bethlehem' is made 'not least' among his compatriots, and geographically clarified. All of which fits into the pattern of Jesus, the Davidic Messiah, who was born in Bethlehem, at least according to this early tradition, but it can hardly be considered an 'objective' reading of Scripture. Similarly, the divergencies of the second example need not be referred back to a variant Hebrew tradition. It is clear that the Old Testament text concerned containing

which we have heard and known, and our fathers have told us

hardly fits in with the doctrine of revealed eschatological knowledge we have just been discussing, and the singular 'parable' has been made plural to apply to Jesus' words. In the last example, Matthew has read his Hebrew quite illegitimately from a literary point of view, possibly in order to make it conform to a current tradition involving two animals.

Now it has long been recognized that such paraphrasing has been practised by the New Testament writers, and there are some parallel usages to be found in rabbinic literature, but in the Dead Sea scrolls we find the same practice and

method used time and time again, and there is no her-
meneutic principle of interpretation in the New Testament
which cannot be exactly matched in the Qumran literature.
There are some very good examples in the Habakkuk Commentary of the writer deliberately altering his text to fit his
interpretation. In Habakkuk i. 13 the prophet is speaking to
the Lord, and says:

Thou that art of purer eyes than to behold evil and that canst not
look upon perverseness.

The commentator interprets this to mean, quite reasonably,
that God will not let His people perish in the hands of the
Gentiles; rather the Gentiles will fall into the hands of the
Elect. But in the next part of the verse,

wherefore lookest Thou upon them that deal treacherously, and
holdest Thy peace when the wicked swalloweth up the man that is
more righteous than he,

whilst the prophet is still, of course, addressing God, the
commentator fastens immediately upon the persecution of
the Teacher by the Wicked Priest theme and makes it ask a
renegade element of the Sect, called the 'House of Absalom',
why they stood by when the righteous Priest suffered. But
to do this, he must change the singular 'lookest Thou' to the
plural 'look ye', and does so in his quotation, although,
needless to say, a plural in the text read consecutively makes
nonsense.

Again in ii. 5, where the prophet is making a personification of wine, 'the treacherous dealer', who

enlargeth his desire as Hell ... and cannot be satisfied,

the commentator writes in his text *hwn*, 'wealth' for Habakkuk's *hyyn* 'the wine', a very slight orthographic change
certainly but giving a very different meaning and according
very well with what he wanted to say about the greed of the
Wicked Priest in contrast to the avowed poverty of the Sect.
Sometimes, the commentator will change the text of his
quotation and then use not only the new version but the old

as well, and derive his interpretation from both! Thus in
ii. 15, a condemnation of the deliberate intoxication of one's
neighbour 'that thou mayest look upon his nakedness', the
word for 'nakedness' has been given a very slight orthographic change and reads 'their seasons'. This does not gives
a particular meaningful sense in the context, but it does
mean that the commentator can play on the 'nakedness' of
the original and introduces a root meaning 'strip' which is
closely similar to another meaning 'exile', from which he
draws the picture of the Teacher being pursued and perse-
cuted in exile, and uses his 'seasons' to bring in the fact that
the persecution took place in the 'season' of rest, the Day of
Atonement.

In other places this astute author finds the words to suit
his commentary not by changing the text but by using a
traditional variant of which he seemed to know, and which
we sometimes have preserved for us in some Targum or
Midrashic work, and will sometimes proceed to use both
traditions in his commentary. He may even split a word and
use its two parts, or, leaving the orthography of the text as it
stands, use more than one meaning for one of the words
involved and comment on both.

Even the New Testament 'compound' quotation is to be
found in Qumran. In a group of prophetic testimonies, for
instance, we find the passage Deuteronomy v. 28–9 run
straight on with the famous prophecy of Deuteronomy
xviii. 18 in such a way as to give an entirely new meaning to
the first text. Thus the Lord says:

I have heard the voice of the words of this people, which they have
spoken unto thee: they have well said all that they have spoken. O
that there were such an heart in them, that they would fear me,
and keep my commandments always, that it might be well with
them, and with their children for ever!

The people, it may be remembered, had been asking for a
mediator between themselves and God, and in the verses
that follow God appoints Moses to that office. But the purpose of these testimonies is to bring together a series of texts

that warn of the fate awaiting those who fail to heed God's messengers in the end-time. Chief of these are, of course, the Messiah and his precursor, the Prophet; and the compiler has no compunction in following an ancient Samaritan tradition and continuing directly with the quotation:

I will raise them up a prophet from among their brethren, like unto thee; and I will put my words in his mouth, and he shall speak unto them all that I shall command him.

Thus the first text no longer refers to Moses, but to the long-awaited Prophet and the divine source of his authority. The second text is, incidentally, referred in the New Testament to Jesus, as in the speeches of Peter and Stephen (Acts iii. 22, vii. 37).

This *testimonia* document from Qumran (pl. 12) is among the most interesting of the works found, and throws new light on a much discussed problem of the early Church. It has been argued since the end of the last century that there existed in the Church from the very beginning collections of Old Testament quotations which were used by the fathers in debate and teaching. This theory has some backing from similar collections in use by the Church of later times, which may well, so it has been argued, be based on much earlier documents. Furthermore such a theory would account for the composite quotations found in the New Testament, the ascription of passages to the wrong biblical writers where a number of variously derived *testimonia* had been placed together under the name of one prophet, and for the textual variants which seem to persist in certain oft-repeated passages. A recent writer has suggested that the groups of such *testimonia* were gathered together under separate headings such as messianic, legal, apocalyptic, and so on. Although the whole theory has not gone unchallenged, it now seems that we have from Qumran important support for the idea in a pre-Christian collection of eschatological *testimonia*, the very first of which is a composite quotation!

Matthew's quotations from the Old Testament fall into two separate groups: those preceded by the formula

Now this is come to pass, that it might be fulfilled which was
spoken by the prophet so-and-so

and the like, and those which are given quite simply without such an introductory phrase or sentence. It has further
been observed that whilst the 'formula quotations' tend to
follow the Hebrew text of the Bible, the non-formula type
agree more with the LXX tradition. It may be no coincid-
ence that this group of unadorned *testimonia* we have been
discussing shows marked 'Greek' tendencies, clearly taken
from a tradition close to that used by the ancient translators.
It seems, therefore, not improbable that certain Jewish
sections of the early Church like the Matthew school were
using very old groups of *testimonia* in a Hebrew of the pre-
Massoretic 'Greek' tradition like so many of our Qumran
biblical texts.

Furthermore, it has long been realized that Stephen's
speech in the seventh chapter of Acts shows remarkable
affinities with the Samaritan recension of the Pentateuch
where it quotes the Old Testament. Now that we know that
at this very time there were copies of this recension circulating in a strict Jewish community like the Qumran Sect, it
seems not improbable that they were also in use by certain
sections of the Church.

CHAPTER ELEVEN

JOHN THE BAPTIST

To most people the association of the River Jordan, baptism, and the call to repentance brings to mind most vividly the figure of John the Baptist. Marked off from his youth for the ascetic life of a prophet, John remained in the deserts of Judaea until 'the time of his showing unto Israel'. His wild, unkempt appearance, his uncompromising call to repentance, and his fanatical assurance of the nearness of the Day of Judgement, made a particular appeal to the people when he finally began his public ministry. He cared for no man and condemned hypocrisy and complacency wherever he found it, to the delight of the ordinary man who had suffered enough from both in the priesthood. There seems to have grown up around him a band of admirers who were later inclined to ascribe to him a messianic role, which, according to the Fourth Gospel, he was most anxious to deny. He was but a messenger,

the voice of one crying in the wilderness,
Make straight the way of the Lord. (John i. 23; cp. Isaiah xl. 3).

John's baptism was for the remission of sins, but that remission depended on a genuine showing of the fruits of repentance, after which alone could the suppliant be purified in the flesh with water. Even this was a preparatory ritual only, for the days were coming when the Messiah himself would baptize, not with water, but

with the Holy Spirit and with fire. (Matthew iii. 11)

Indeed, the eschatological process had already begun,

even now the axe is laid unto the root of the trees, (Matthew iii. 10).

and thoughts of personal wealth and prestige could be put aside for ever. Now was the time to share one's worldly goods, to live honestly, and in quiet expectation of the end.

The Qumran Community quoted the same Isaianic passage to describe their own work of preparation, which was to study the Law and abide by the teachings of Moses and the prophets. They also demanded true repentance before baptism, and likewise promised a further cleansing by God.

through the Holy Spirit ... sprinkling upon him a Spirit of Truth as purifying as water.

As we know, the Sect believed in the approach of the Day of Visitation and that this period of preparation would not allow of the accumulation of personal wealth, and they practised communal ownership of property.

Yet for all the similarities in their respective teachings, John was clearly at this time not of the Qumran Community. His mixing with the common man and thus separation from the 'Purity of the Many' would make his continued membership of the Community impossible. Theirs was no evangelistic call to mankind, but an esoteric Community of the Elect. Whilst others could join, it was only after a rigorous period of self-denial and probation. It does appear, however, that John may have belonged to the Essene movement, and correspondences with Qumran doctrine could easily be explained on the basis of their possessing many ideas and documents which were common to the Essene Sect as a whole. One interesting suggestion has been advanced that John had been adopted by the Qumran Sect as a boy, and this would certainly account for his being in the deserts at such an early age. We have already seen that some branches of the Essenes eschewed marriage, and to keep up their number adopted other people's children

whilst yet pliable and docile, and regarded them as their kin and moulded them in accordance with their own principles.

As the son of a priest he would have been welcomed by such a Community and probably marked out for a leading role in the Sect. When we meet him he is no longer a member, which may suggest expulsion, or voluntary resignation, perhaps when he received this overwhelming conviction of the need to take his message to the common people. We are told that besides his wearing of only the simplest garments, he ate only honey and locusts, both of which are mentioned in the food laws at the end of the *Damascus Document*. This again may indicate that the food he was able to eat was strictly limited owing to his purity vows taken in the Community.

Whether this theory be in accordance with the facts or not, it is certain that John the Baptist and his disciples exercised a very considerable influence on Jesus and the Church, and it is equally certain that much of John's message finds its parallels in Qumran teaching.

CHAPTER TWELVE

THE QUMRAN COMMUNITY AND
THE CHURCH

Doctrinal Affinities

FROM a very early stage, the Church seems to have been known as 'those of the Way' or 'the Way of God', which was recognized as a distinct sect (Acts xxiv. 14). This same term is used of the Qumran Covenanters, who, according to the *Manual*, are 'those who choose the Way'. Furthermore, both groups describe themselves as The Poor Ones, the Children of Light, the Elect of God, a Community of the *New Testament* or *Covenant*. The eighth chapter of the Epistle to the Hebrews quotes in full the Jeremiah passage which is behind this conception, and goes on to describe the Church as a new Temple of God where sacrificial redemption is made once for all for the world. And the Qumran Sect describes itself as

an eternal planting, a holy house of Israel, a most holy conclave for Aaron, witnesses of Truth in judgement, and chosen by divine favour to atone for the land, to render to the wicked their deserts. This is the tried wall, the precious corner stone, whose foundation shall not be shaken nor moved from its place.

Extraordinarily similar is Peter's description of the Church:

ye also, as living stones, are built up a spiritual house to be a holy priesthood, to offer up spiritual sacrifices, acceptable to God through Jesus Christ. Because it is contained in Scripture, Behold, I lay in Zion a chief corner stone, elect, precious ... But ye are an elect race, a royal priesthood, a holy nation, a people of *God's* own possession ... (I. ii. 5–9).

Both the Sect and the Christian Church believe they have been given a share in the inheritance of the angels, or holy ones, and both communities see themselves as founded by a Teacher at the command of God, to execute a judgement on the earth at the end of days.

For the Qumran Sect the expiation of the iniquity of Israel is achieved by

> practising justice, and the anguish of the refining furnace.

Never far from the conception of this righteous remnant, the True Israel, is the theme of suffering; the oft-referred-to persecution of the Teacher of Righteousness is usually accompanied by the mention of 'his Party', and allusions to the Suffering Servant of Isaiah seem explicit in such phrases as 'witnesses of Truth in judgement' mentioned above, and after the parallel

> Ye are my witnesses, saith the Lord, and my Servant whom I have chosen

in the Servant song of Isaiah (xliii. 10). In one of their hymns, the Sect pictures itself as a pregnant woman suffering the pangs of parturition as she gives birth to her 'firstborn', who is described in terms reminiscent of the Child of Isaiah ix. 6, the 'Wonderful Counsellor'.

Most scholars agree that the passage retains its biblical messianic significance, in which case it appears that the Sect believed that out of its suffering of atonement for 'the land' would come the Anointed One or Christ. Whether the 'land' for which atonement is made extended beyond the confines of Judaism is open to question. One naturally assumes not; on the face of it the extension of messianic privileges to the non-Jewish world would have seemed as heterodox to this Jewish group as it did to Paul's opponents among the Jewish leaders of the Church in Jerusalem. Nevertheless, the germ of the idea of Israel's universal mission is already present in the Old Testament. Thus in the Servant Songs of Isaiah:

It is too light a thing that thou shouldest be my Servant,
    to restore the tribes of Jacob,
and lead back the remnant of Israel;
    I have made thee a light to the Gentiles
that my salvation may reach to the end of the earth (xlix. 6);

and in xlii. 6:

I have made thee for a covenant of the people, a light to the
Gentiles.

And whilst scholars may debate the vexed question of
whether Jesus really intended the non-Jewish world to
share in the Kingdom (the New Testament evidence is self-
contradictory on the matter), the intention of the author of
the following Qumran hymn seems clear:

I take comfort when the peoples roar
and the nations are in tumult,
    for in a little while I know
that Thou wilt raise up survivors among Thy people,
    and a remnant in Thine inheritance;
and Thou shalt purify them,
    to cleanse them from guilt:
for all their deeds (were wrought) in Thy truth,
    and in Thy lovingkindness Thou wilt judge them ...

For Thy glory and for Thine own sake Thou hast acted,
    that [...] the Law,
and [Thou hast sent (?)] the men of Thy counsel
    amongst the sons of men
to recount Thy wonders to everlasting generations
    and Thy mighty deeds without end:
that all nations may know Thy truth
and all peoples Thy glory.

Formal Affinities

The Community of Qumran as a whole is given the technical
connotation of 'The Many', and is democratically governed
by such deliberative councils as we saw described in

Chapter 7. This term appears in its literal translation in the New Testament, and describes the Jerusalem Council of Acts xv. 12 (RV: 'multitude'), the body of the disciples who appointed the Seven (Acts vi. 2, 5), and the congregation of the Antioch Church (Acts xv. 30). It has, as we have seen, been suggested also that the office of 'Bishop' in the Church has its origin in the Qumran 'Overseer'.

There has long been recognized in the Gospel of Matthew a certain ordering of his material which suggests something in the nature of a handbook for the early Church. It is carefully arranged into five sections, adopts a casuistry in its teaching of moral principles which is almost legal, and has much to say on the position and duties of the Church leaders. A good instance of this method of ordering material on moral discipline is the passage in xviii. 15–17, where the procedure for complaints between the brethren is dealt with and put into the mouth of Jesus. First, reproof is to be made on a personal basis; failing satisfaction, it is to be made before one or two witnesses, and if the wrongdoer is still unrepentant, before the whole Church. Only then, if still recalcitrant, may he be banished from the Community. The *Manual* shows the same regulation for the Qumran Sect:

Let no one speak to his brother in anger, or in grumbling complaint, or with obstinate pride [. . . or] evil spirit; nor shall he hate him [. . .] of his heart, although he may reprove him at that time so as not to incur guilt because of him. Indeed, no man may bring a case against his fellow before the Many which has not first been the subject of a reproof before witnesses.

We saw that the method of priests of the Qumran Community giving their casting vote was by the casting of 'lots'. It will be remembered that this procedure was used in the early Church for finding a replacement for the defaulting Judas:

And they gave lots for them; and the lot fell upon Matthias; and he was numbered with the eleven disciples (Acts i. 26).

Another correspondence of procedure in both communities is in the pooling of their possessions once they had entered the brotherhood. Deliberate falsification of one's declaration in this respect was a particularly heinous sin in Qumran, as it was in the Church, as we gather from the story of Ananias and Sapphira in Acts v. 1–11.

Whilst on the subject of money, new light on a rather puzzling incident recorded of Jesus in the New Testament has come from a Qumran document. Matthew tells us that Peter was one day accosted by tax-collectors demanding to know if his master paid the customary half-shekel required annually of every Jew aged twenty and over (xvii. 24–7). Peter hastily affirmed that he did, but it is clear from what Jesus says afterwards that in fact he felt no obligation to do so. We now know that the Qumran Sect required of its members payment of this Temple tax *only once in a lifetime*. If Jesus had been brought up to this rule he would have already paid the half-shekel and thus felt himself exonerated from further payment.

We have already referred to another practice of the Qumran Community which has its important parallel in the Church, the Messianic Banquet, or Lord's Supper. We have seen that ideally it is attended by the High Priest, or priestly Messiah, his Davidic counterpart, and the whole Congregation of Israel under their elders and sages. That Jesus was well acquainted with the idea has long been recognized, not only through his parables of the Banquet but in the incidents of crowd-feeding by the Sea of Galilee, which are but an earthly anticipation of the Messianic Feast. The Last Supper of Jesus is again clearly connected in his mind with the coming heavenly Banquet:

for I say unto you, I will not drink from henceforth of the fruit of the vine until the Kingdom of God shall come ... I appoint unto you a kingdom, even as my Father appointed unto me, that ye may eat and drink at my table in my kingdom; and ye shall sit on thrones judging the twelve tribes of Israel (Luke xxii. 18, 29–30).

A curious point of the gospel narrative appears in a revealing light through the Qumran *Rule*. Luke records that after the Supper there arose a contention among them which of them is accounted to be the greatest (xxii. 24).

Now in the *Rule*, the seating and serving of the participants of the Messianic Banquet was strictly according to their respective ranks in the kingdom. If Jesus and His disciples are observing this Qumran ritual, the disputing of the twelve about precedence is clearly occasioned by their order of seating, not as a matter of petty pride, but because their position in the heavenly kingdom was concerned. Although we read that Jesus sharply rebukes this preoccupation with rank, and thus apparently upsets the established form of ritual, the Lucan account goes on then to this promise of a place at the true Messianic Feast, and of the twelve thrones in the new Kingdom.

It need hardly be added that the Qumran ritual knows nothing of any words of institution allegorizing the bread and wine of the Meal as the body and blood of a messianic sacrifice, or even more remotely, of seeing in them a means of 'participation in the body of (the) Christ' (I Corinthians x. 16). These latter sentiments at least are far removed from Palestinian Judaism.

Jesus' Last Supper is connected by the Synoptic Gospels with the Jewish Passover feast (Matthew xxvi. 17, Mark xiv. 12, Luke xxii. 7). But according to John xix. 14, Jesus' trial before Pilate and crucifixion took place at that time. This apparently unresolvable contradiction in the timing of events of Passion Week has been tackled anew by scholars on the basis of the Qumran calendar (see Chapter 7). We know that the Qumran Covenanters would have been celebrating Passover on Tuesday night, for it will be remembered that by their calendar reckoning the feast days would fall on the same day of the week each year. If Jesus and his followers had been following this sectarian practice, they too would have been partaking of their meal on the Tuesday night. There would thus have been ample time for the arrest and trial before the day of Preparation, Friday, according to the official calendar which John would seem to be using for his account of the events. This is certainly an attractive suggestion for a way out of the chronological difficulty, and is not without its support in ancient Judaeo-Christian tradition. But needless to say, it has run into strong opposition in some quarters which would not relish the idea of Jesus being quite so closely connected with the Qumran sect as this would imply.

A more reasonable argument is that we have no other case recorded in the New Testament where Jesus appears to run counter to the official observance of the Jewish festivals in which he is reported as taking part. However, the real point at issue is probably whether we can trust the Gospel records on such matters of detail as the day-to-day events of a single week, or even in their identification of the Lord's Supper with the Jewish Passover which the majority of their Gentile readers would not understand anyway.

CHAPTER THIRTEEN

THE MESSIANIC CONCEPTIONS
OF QUMRAN AND THE
EARLY CHURCH

THE Qumran Sect looked to the coming of a Priestly Messiah or Christ ('Anointed One'), whom they call 'Teacher of Righteousness' and 'Interpreter of the Law'. The fact that these are precisely the terms they apply to the priestly founder of the Sect suggests the idea that it may have been their resurrected Teacher who would lead the theocratic community of the New Israel in the Last Days.

This new Kingdom was essentially a holy institution, a congregation of saints devoted to the service of God and the study of His Law. To the Covenanters, the onset of the new order would mean a continuation of the pious existence they were then leading, for the whole idea of their present way of life was that it should be a rehearsal of the messianic age. But, then, their communion with God would be complete, for any difficulties in the interpretation of the Law, or questions concerning their way of life, could be referred to their messianic Teacher of Righteousness, the perfect mediator between Man and God.

This, then, was the priestly Messiah, but it is now clear that along with him they expected the appearance of another, lay, Anointed One, a Prince of the line of David. It is not, perhaps, surprising that it was some time before scholars realized that phrases like 'the Messiah of Aaron and Israel' in Qumran literature, actually meant 'the Messiah of Aaron *and the Messiah* of Israel', many having taken the one instance where we find the plural 'the Messiahs of Aaron and Israel' as a scribal error or the like.

However, once the idea of two Messiahs had been considered at all feasible, correspondences were found in
Jewish thought both before and after the Qumran period,
which showed that the idea was not, after all, so very unique.
The origins seem to go back to the breaking down of the old
theocracy of Israel, when both secular and spiritual power
was in the hands of the High Priest. There arose a secular
political régime, often in conflict with the religious interests
of the nation and the two arms of government drew farther
and farther apart. With the patterning of the messianic on
the temporal order, the need for both sides to be represented
in the new era was envisaged, and even as early as the
end of the sixth century, we see both the Aaronic High
Priest and the Davidic prince referred to as 'the anointed',
literally 'sons of oil' (Zechariah iv. 14). With the loss of independence, the title of King naturally lapsed, and it was
not until Hasmonean times that the two offices were united
by the High Priest's adoption of the title of King, an act of
usurpation which shocked the pious Israelite of the time.
However, the idea of the dual messianic office continued at
least until the time of the Second Revolt (A.D. 132–5), for
the coins of that time speak of El'azar the High Priest, side
by side with Shim'on bar Kochebah, the Prince of Israel
(pl. 8b).

We have already seen that at the Messianic Banquet des-
scribed in the *Manual*, both the High Priest and the Messiah
of Israel are mentioned, and another document refers to
them both as arising together at the end of time. The
Davidic Messiah is really a war leader and judge, and in
the blessing upon him recorded in the *Manual*, it is said
that

he will renew for Him the Covenant of the Community (charging
him) to establish the kingdom of His people for ev[er, to judge the
poor justly, and] to reprove with e[quity the hum]ble of the land,
to walk before Him in perfection, in all the ways of [...], and to
restore His [holy all]iance [in] the time of distress with all those
who ·eek [Him. May] the Lord li[ft th]ee up to an everlasting
height like a fortified tower on a high wall, that thou [mightest

smite the peoples] with the might of thy [mouth], with thy
sceptre devastate the land, and with the breath of thy lips kill the
wick[ed, armed with the spirit of cou]nsel and everlasting might,
the spirit of knowledge, and the fear of God. And righteousness
shall be the girdle [of thy loins, and fai]th the belt of thy reins.
[And] may He make thy horns of iron and thy hooves of brass to
gore like a young bu[ll ... and tread down the peop]les like the
mire of the streets. For God has established thee as a sceptre over
rulers. Bef[ore thee shall they come and do obeisance, and all the
nat]ions will serve thee, and by His holy name He will strengthen
thee. And thou shalt be like a l[ion ...] prey with none to resto[re],
and thy [mess]engers will spread over [the face of the earth ...

The Davidic Messiah, then, is the warrior of God, the
holy instrument by which He will restore the kingdom of
His people, and protect the pious poor who seek to know
Him. And it is with this lay Messiah that we may expect
to find correspondences with Christian ideas. Like the
Qumran Messiah, Jesus was expected to 'kill the wicked
with the breath of his lips' (cp. 2 Thessalonians ii. 8), and
the inscription which the soldiers nailed above his cross
'King of the Jews' possibly bears a mocking allusion to the
messianic title 'Prince of Israel', used not only of the Davidic Messiah in Qumran literature but of bar Kochebah
later on. The word for 'prince', *nāsî*, means 'one lifted up'
and Jesus may be playing on this idea in his prophecy:

... as Moses lifted up the serpent in the wilderness, even so must
the Son of Man be lifted up (John iii. 14, cp. viii. 28, xii. 32, 34).

with an added allusion to the manner of his death.

In the New Testament we learn that the great apocalyptic
war of the 'kings of the whole world' was to take place at
Armageddon, generally regarded as the graecized form of
the Hebrew *har-megiddo*, 'the hill (or hill-country) of
Megiddo' (Revelation xvi. 16, cp. Zechariah xii. 11). This
city was the fortress which guarded the vital pass opening
out from the south into the plain of Esdraelon, or Jezreel,
the scene of so many battles in Israel's history. Now, from
Qumran, we have confirmation of this identification, for a

fragmentary commentary on Isaiah, concerned mainly with eschatological events, describes the progress of the antichrist and his forces in terms of Isaiah's dramatic picture of the approach of the hostile Assyrians towards Jerusalem (x. 28–32). 'He will go up,' says our commentator, 'from Accho'. This valley can be readily identified with the coastal plain through which a road ran down from Ptolemais, or *Accho*, into the Jezreel plain from the west.

The hills of Galilee which border this plain were famed as the base of operations for outlawry of all kinds, offering as they did ample protection in their caves to which the rebellious bands could retire after their raids. Part of the Judaeo-Christian Church was centred in this area, and, of course, this was the traditional home of Jesus of Nazareth.

The Scrolls and the New Testament have given a similar messianic interpretation to a number of Old Testament passages. Among the better known is Isaiah xi. 1:

And there shall come forth a shoot out of the stock of Jesse (cp. Acts xiii. 22f.).

Like Paul, the Covenanters saw in the 'shoot' of David, son of Jesse, the coming Messiah, ordained for the salvation of Israel, and it was for this that Jesus received his name which in its Hebrew form 'Joshua' embodies the idea of 'save' (Matthew i. 21).

In the order of the Messianic Banquet it is said that God would 'beget' the Davidic Messiah, and in a Qumran document dealing with the re-establishment of the Kingdom of David in the Last Days, the prophecy of II Samuel vii. 13–14:

I will establish the throne of his kingdom for ever.
I will be his father and he shall be my son

is referred to the same figure, as it is in the New Testament (Hebrew i. 5). We appear, then, to have in Qumran thought already the idea of the lay Messiah as the Son of God, 'begotten' of the Father, a 'Saviour' in Israel. At the same time, we nowhere approach the 'christology' of Paul in the Scrolls, or the kind of divinity accorded Jesus by the Greek Church. And needless to say the Jewish Covenanters nowhere press the idea of the divinely begotten son-Messiah and a co-existent Holy Spirit to any doctrine of a trinitarian godhead as was done by Greek Christianity.

The writer of the Epistle to the Hebrews, in the course of his argument, quotes Psalm xlv. 6–7, one of the 'coronation psalms' of the Old Testament. Our Qumran commentator on Isaiah also has this passage in mind when he pictures the Messiah as seated on his 'throne of glory', and receiving not only his 'holy crown' and 'garments of variegated stuff' from the hands of 'priests of repute', but even his exacting standards of judgement: 'as they teach him so shall he judge'.

One cannot help wondering if, in this current idea of the training of the young Messiah, we have not the origin of the strangely isolated story in the New Testament of Jesus receiving instruction at the feet of the doctors in the Temple (Luke ii. 41–50). Be that as it may, it is noticeable that in the messianic hierarchy as well as in the institution of the Qumran sect we have the priest taking precedence over the layman. Again, this is well demonstrated in the order for the Messianic Banquet, where the priests must be seated before the Davidic Messiah may enter with his followers. Nobody must touch the bread and wine before the High Priest has laid his hands upon them and distributed them to his priests. Only then may the Davidic Messiah do the same for his company of laymen.

Whether the Sectarians ever reached the stage in their thinking when they merged the two functions of the messianic office into one person, we cannot say for certain, for want of evidence. Such a unification is not without its difficulties, as the writer to the Hebrews in the New Testament points out in his description of Jesus as messianic High Priest. He tries to explain to his Jewish-Christian readers (thought by some scholars, on the basis of a number of correspondences between the Epistle and the scrolls, to have been Essenes in general or even the Qumran group in particular) how Jesus, born of the line of David, a non-priestly family, could undertake these duties:

For the priesthood being changed, there is made of necessity a change also of the law. For he of whom these things are said belongeth to another tribe, from which no man hath given attendance at the altar. For it is evident that our Lord hath sprung out of Judah; as to which tribe Moses spake nothing concerning priests (vii. 12–14).

He therefore concludes that Jesus, the Davidic Messiah, has been given a special priesthood of a unique order, surpassing that of the old Aaronic line, and patterned after the ancient priest-king, Melchizedek. In Jesus, the various functions of both Messiahs have been combined.

CHAPTER FOURTEEN

JESUS AND THE SCROLLS

In any new field of comparative literary studies there is a tendency to overstrain the evidence. Scholars are apt to find parallels in thought, even direct borrowing, where the similarities are more probably due to a common fund of human experience, or even to the natural limitations of literary communication. The study of the scrolls has suffered from this tendency as much as, if not more than, other disciplines. This is particularly so where the New Testament is the object of comparison, for undoubtedly this aspect of the discoveries has received the greatest attention.

Nevertheless, there have been positive results which point to a correspondence in outlook between the scrolls and the New Testament that must go deeper than their common heritage of Judaism and the Old Testament. On the whole, these parallels are in fields of specialist research not readily accessible or comprehensible to the layman. The point at which the inquiry does touch upon a common sphere of interest is in the person of Jesus of Nazareth. But it is just here that emotional factors tend to influence judgement most, and where the issues have been obscured by special pleading from all sides.

When the scrolls first became world news, parallels were popularly drawn between Jesus and the Essene Teacher of Righteousness which were either not in themselves valid or were given a wholly disproportionate amount of publicity, not least by those who rejected them. With the apparent intention of calming the fears of Christian laymen that the uniqueness of the faith was in jeopardy, a number of scholars devoted papers, tracts, and even books to the object of persuading people that there were many differences between the Teacher and Jesus, and that the Christian Master could not be linked too closely with the Essene or any other sectarian movement within Judaism. Whilst admitting there are interesting parallels in thought between the scrolls and the New Testament, these scholars have been at great pains to list the essential differences in outlook. Thus, for example, the bitterness displayed by the scrolls in their attitude towards those outside their sect is contrasted with the love Jesus showed towards sinners; the eschatology of the scrolls with its emphasis upon the fearful holocaust that would precede the coming of the new era is contrasted with those words of Jesus which speak of the Kingdom growing within a person. The ascetic nature of the Qumran mode of living is set against the picture of Jesus mixing with wine-bibbers and gluttons. The fleeting euphemistic references to the death of the Teacher of Righteousness are contrasted with the prominence given in the New Testament to the crucifixion of Jesus and its religious import for the Church. The reverence offered the deceased Teacher by the Essenes is set against the worship of the Risen Lord among Christians as to God Himself. Nowhere, it is said, does the Scrolls Community speak unequivocally of their Teacher as Messiah, whereas recognition of Jesus as the Christ was a fundamental tenet of the Christian faith. And so on.

Whatever effect these arguments had on the disquieted laity, they contributed very little to the speculation among disinterested observers on what, if anything, the scrolls told us about the man Jesus and his place in history. The intelligent reader quickly realized that what these apologetics were contrasting was not two historical persons but two quite different worlds of thought. On the one hand there was the priestly leader of an extremist Jewish sect seen through the eyes of his followers; on the other the image of a Jewish rabbi transmitted through the Greek writings of a predominantly non-Jewish Church intent on making him and his message acceptable to the Gentile world. The wonder is that sufficient of the original remains identifiable to allow comparison to be made at all.

The fact is that we know very little about the man Jesus or his background. The sayings attributed to him in the New

Testament are mostly in translation, out of context, and full of allusions to a lost world of Jewish sectarianism of which even now we are hardly aware. Here and there the scrolls have enabled us to pick up a word or phrase which for the first time can be given its original import, but we have to acknowledge that a great deal has been lost in translation or early misunderstanding, perhaps irrevocably.

Readers will understand, therefore, that in our present state of ignorance it is not easy to assess Jesus' place in the Jewish world of his day and thus to what extent the scrolls can throw light on his religious background. We can certainly assume that he would have been acquainted with Essenism, since from all accounts it was widespread throughout Palestine. As we have seen, some of the scrolls seem to have more revelance for urban Essenism than the ascetic life of the Qumran monastery. There must however have been considerable differences between these two branches of the movement, and Jesus would have been better acquainted with Essenes in the towns and villages than those in such monastic communities as Qumran. We should need to know a lot more about urban Essenism before we could be dogmatic on how close were Jesus' affinities with this sect.

My own opinion is that the scrolls prompt us increasingly to seek an eschatological meaning for most of Jesus' reported sayings: more and more become intelligible when viewed in the light of the imminent cataclysm of Qumran expectations, and the inner conflict in men's hearts as the time drew near.

As far as details in the New Testament record of Jesus' life are concerned, I would suggest that the scrolls give added ground for believing that many incidents are merely projections into Jesus' own history of what was expected of the Messiah. Had we more knowledge of these expectations, even for instance the remainder of the fragmentary commentary on Isaiah which deals with the training and coronation of the Davidic Messiah, we might well be able to pin down the origin of a number of other New Testament myths.

To sum up, at the end of the day we may have to admit that the main contribution of the Dead Sea scrolls to modern thought has been to remind us how ignorant we are still about the events and opinions of sectarian Judaism at the turn of the era. If this conclusion seems disappointingly negative, it is nevertheless true that the light the scrolls have managed to throw on to this crucial period in man's history has brought some illumination where before was almost total darkness. It has at least dispelled a number of false assumptions and opened the way to the reception of new ideas, or perhaps the rehabilitation of ideas prematurely abandoned because they did not suit our preconceptions.

Clearing away the deadwood is the first condition of intellectual progress; but whether this generation has courage or vision to grasp the opportunities of reassessment offered by these miraculous discoveries in the Judaean wilderness, remains to be seen.

OTHER CAVE DISCOVERIES OF HISTORY AND AFFILIATIONS WITH THE QUMRAN SECT

AT some time about the beginning of the ninth century of our era, a Syrian Metropolitan of Seleucia, Timotheus, writing to his superior, recounted an incident which had been told him by some Jewish proselytes from Jerusalem. It seems that, about ten years before, an Arab shepherd boy had been searching for a lost animal near Jericho and had stumbled upon a cave, and, climbing in, had discovered some ancient scrolls. He had told some Jews in Jerusalem who went down and cleared many more scrolls, finding that they were written in Hebrew and in an old script, and contained biblical and other works. Timotheus suggested that the cache had been placed there by Jeremiah and Baruch before the Exile, which may indicate that his informants had told him that the scrolls had been found in jars, with which he had connected the 'earthen vessel' of Jeremiah xxxii. 14. In any case, Timotheus says that he himself was most interested in whether these scrolls contained Old Testament texts in the variant forms in which they appear in the New Testament, but save for hearing that they were so represented in the scrolls, he was unable to gain further information.

We have already seen in Chapter 7 that Karaite and Muslim writers of the tenth–twelfth centuries were speaking of a Cave Sect, so called because their documents had been discovered in a cave, and we noted that the calendar used by this sect seems to correspond with that favoured by the Qumran Covenanters and found in the book of Jubilees.

Furthermore, the *Damascus Document*, of which we have had occasion to speak previously, was first known to modern scholarship in medieval copies found at the end of the last century in an ancient Karaite synagogue in Cairo. Although dated palaeographically to the tenth and twelfth centuries A.D., it was soon recognized that their contents stemmed from a very much earlier period, and the discovery of fragmentary copies in the Qumran caves occasioned no great surprise. But scholars have noted that Karaite literature of the ninth and tenth centuries begins to show remarkable correspondences with Qumran writings. At this time, words and expressions previously absent from the literature of this Jewish sect over the preceding centuries begin to appear. For example, the title 'Teacher of Righteousness' does not appear before the ninth-century commentary on Joel by an author of the Sect. Furthermore, from the second half of the ninth century until the tenth, the underlying antagonism between the Karaite sect of Jews and the orthodox Rabbanites suddenly flares up in a new burst of polemic activity. There are constant references to the 'Zadokite' sect and its doctrine in the literature of this period, and the writings of the group appear to have had a wide circulation, being 'well known among the people', according to a Karaite author. Furthermore, the Rabbanites of Jerusalem of the tenth century themselves began to adopt religious practices which were by no means the custom in Talmudic circles. Thus they became partly vegetarians, avoided cooked food, olive oil, honey, and, indeed, any food likely to contain 'crawling things' or other impurities. They applied strictly the law of levitical purity, not allowing the marriage with a niece or stepsister. Most interestingly, in view of what we have said about the calendar, they began to duplicate the observation of religious festivals, fixing the one set by observation and the other by the old traditional system of calendation. The tenth-century Karaite author who tells us this says that they borrowed these practices from his own sect. Certainly many of the new customs are to be found promoted in Karaite writings, and some of the dietary restrictions and levitical laws of purity approximate to what we find in the legal section of the *Damascus Document*.

All these lines of evidence leave little doubt that at the end of the ninth century a startling discovery of manuscripts, which bear many important resemblances to those from the Qumran library, was made similarly in a cave near Jericho. The documents must have been assiduously copied and taken into circulation, with a considerable effect on all those who came into contact with them. The Karaites seem to have found in them much which accorded with their own ideals, which might throw some interesting new light on the origins of this important Jewish sectarian movement. But even the orthodox Rabbanites seem to have recognized a note of authority in these writings which made them adopt a double calendar and unfamiliar food and purity laws.

MURABBA'AT AND OTHER SITES

IT was not until January 1952 that an official excavation of the Murabba'at caves (Chapter 2) was made, and once more the Jordanian Department of Antiquities under Gerald Harding, and the French School of Archaeology led by Father De Vaux undertook the task. The main difficulty of this excavation was that of supplies, since the rains were still falling and stores had to be brought by mule and donkey the whole seven-hour march from Bethlehem as far as the cliffs in which the caves were situated, and then down the last dizzy slopes on human backs.

The Wady Murabba'at or Darajeh is a great gorge, starting under the name of Wady Ta'amireh, east of Bethlehem, almost sheer on its north side and sloping steeply on the south, until, as it enters the Dead Sea, the sides are almost vertical (see map on p. 8). The caves are on the north side of the gorge, at this point some eight hundred feet deep, and about fifteen miles south-east of Jerusalem and eleven miles south of the First Cave of Qumran, as the crow flies. Two of them stand together in the vertical cliff face, a third lies some forty yards to the west, and a fourth some two hundred yards to the east of the others. In front of the grouped caves there runs a narrow rock ledge which provided just enough room for a number of two-man tents. Whilst most convenient for the work, this spot lost some of its attractiveness when it rained, as the water streaming down the slope was apt to loosen large rocks *en route* and send them crashing into the camp. One member had left his tent only a few minutes before a boulder crashed through the roof and smashed into his pillow. The next night he spent in the cave.

Cave One is really a long tunnel running into the mountain-side. The ceiling had collapsed in the remote past, and the first levels of occupation were found on top of the collapsed stones. The roof of the Second Cave, however, had only partially collapsed, almost completely blocking the doorway, so that the first task was to break up the huge boulders and roll them down the cliff face. Unfortunately, the primitive delight which the sight of large rocks crashing their way down hundreds of feet of vertical mountain-side usually engenders in the hearts of children and archaeologists, was somewhat tempered by the knowledge that all the noise going on might shift the remainder of the roof of the cave, hanging precariously above the workers. Every stroke of the foreman's hammer as it crashed into the large slabs of rock, therefore, made the party look anxiously aloft, ready to spring to safety at any sign of movement.

If these hazards were not enough, it soon became evident as the men cleared away the largest boulders that the excavators would have to include pot-holing among their activities, for the narrow crevices revealed led far down into the bowels of the mountain. The most persistent difficulty of the early days, however, showed itself within the first ten minutes of their beginning work. So much of the fine grey dust was kicked up in that time by the workmen that all the pressure lamps became clogged and went out. The team had to fall back on the smoking paraffin flares which the Bedouin had been using. The atmosphere soon became almost unbreathable, but at least there was a murky light to work by.

It was with one of these flares that Harding and a Ta'amireh workman undertook their first burrowing expedition. The workman went in front with the torch and Harding crawled behind, half choked by the fumes of the oil and the dust raised by his companion. However they made fair progress for about fifty feet when suddenly both flare and bearer disappeared. One moment the Bedouin was there raising clouds of dust behind him and the next he was gone, leaving Jordan's Director of Antiquities completely in the dark, scared, as he freely admits, out of his wits, and one workman in Sheol. However, after a little while a voice cried to Allah out of the depths, the flare was relit and the son of the desert climbed out of the pit into which he had fallen, apparently none the worse for his adventure. Later on the lighting situation was saved, thanks to the ready assistance of the Arab Air Force who supplied a portable generator for the use of the expedition. But even that raised grave difficulties, for the heavy parts had to be carried down to the scene of operations on human backs, down tracks which even the loaded mules would not attempt. On another occasion, in the Third Cave, investigation disclosed a great crack in the rock at the back of the cave going down into the depths of the mountain. The Bedouin said that one of their number had already explored it, but to be sure, the foreman of Harding's party, one Hasan Awad, probably the best archaeological foreman in Jordan, volunteered to go down into the crevice on a rope himself. The opening was only two and a half feet wide, and some way down was an even narrower chimney through which he could barely squeeze. Altogether he dropped some fifty feet before landing on a sandy floor, which bore traces of the earlier visit by the Bedouin, but nothing of archaeological value. The haul up was a nightmare for all concerned, as, having no pulleys, the party at the surface had to haul Hasan up, inch by inch, trusting that the rope would not break or be cut by a sharp projection of rock. The half an hour that it took to bring him to the surface seemed like half a day, and the bravery displayed by this man cannot be accounted too highly. Its recounting here may serve to underline the tremendous difficulties under which these archaeologists were working here and in Qumran to the north, and should demonstrate something of the cost at which these priceless Dead Sea scrolls were won.

At the front of the First Cave was a large Roman cistern, carefully lined with plaster, with steps leading down into it, and, in front, a small settling tank. How the water was led into it remains a mystery. The cistern had once been covered, the roof constructed corbel fashion with large flat stones after the fashion of the many such Roman cisterns to be found all along the route to Bethlehem. Long after the rains have ceased the Bedouin can find water in them for themselves and their flocks.

But deeper excavations showed that these caves had been used by man long before the time of the Romans. In all of them sherds were found dating from the Chalcolithic period, about 4000–3000 B.C. In Cave Two, the purely chalcolithic stratum was found sealed by the rocks which obstructed the entrance, and in the lower galleries was found the same layer, about fourteen inches thick, giving directly on to virgin soil, and itself covered by a layer almost as thick of red earth and stones before the debris of later occupations. Flint tools were found in this layer, sickle and other blades, javelin heads, a large scraper, etc., as well as polishers, pierced buttons, and a flat ring of very hard red limestone. There were bone instruments like awls and pointed blades, but the most incredible discoveries in this six-thousand-year-old layer were the wooden objects. These included a donkey goad, which, had the archaeologists not been there when it was discovered, they might have thought had been cut only the day before by the workmen.

Of the same period, but recovered earlier on by the Arabs, was a perfectly preserved haft of an adze, with its polished handle and even the leather thongs for holding the flint blade in position, all in perfect order (pl. 7a). This wonderful state of preservation is due, of course, to the complete protection the inmost recesses of these caves enjoy from the elements and the drying influence of the terrific heat in this area for many months in the year.

Also from Cave Two were discovered the remains of a Middle Bronze Age settlement, both in the upper chamber and in the galleries. Besides the pottery were found two bronze needles, a leather sandal (pl. 7b), and a small alabaster vase. Absolute evidence for dating is happily provided by a scarab decorated with the classical motifs of the Hyksos period. No evidence of a long occupation was forthcoming, but it could mean that in the second part of the Middle Bronze Age, towards the eighteenth and seventeenth centuries, a small human group, or even a few individuals, sojourned in this cave. Probably then, as certainly in later times, these caves offered a refuge from danger during troubled times.

Caves One, Two, and Three all yielded remains of Iron Age occupation, pottery indicating habitation between the eighth and seventh centuries B.C. But the use of the caves was most intense in the Roman period, particularly in the first two caves. Pottery, though fragmentary, was abundant and clearly Roman, and the lamps can be dated quite precisely to the end of the second century of our era. Many metal objects were found, the heads of picks and javelins, generally of bronze, arrow heads of iron, one in the laurel leaf form, and many with three edges. Among the utensils were knives, one of which had its handle of wood quite intact, a sickle, nails, a spatula, a hook, needles of different shapes, and an angular key. Wooden objects were plentiful and included bowls and plates of turned wood, combs, buttons, and spoons. There was a great variety of fabrics, mostly the remains of clothing, often very patched but delicately embroidered. Leather remains included sandals and other equipment. Again evidence was forthcoming for a definite dating of this occupation, for a score of coins appeared, the most numerous being those of the Second Jewish Revolt of A.D. 132–5.

The written documents came almost entirely from the Second Cave. A few are fairly well preserved, but most had suffered from the depredations of visiting animals, human and otherwise, and particularly in the activities of rats who, with a regrettable lack of appreciation of true values, had used the precious leather and papyrus manuscripts as linings for their nests. In fact, the excavation developed into a hunt for rats' nests, since each one was almost sure to produce remnants of a written document or two. Another contributory factor in the denudation of written material was that the later habitation by birds and small animals of the caves over hundreds of years had resulted in an abundant supply of guano which the Bedouin had for years been collecting and selling in Bethlehem. It is not at all improbable, as Father De Vaux points out, that the Jewish orange groves near Bethlehem were fertilized with priceless ancient manuscripts written by their forefathers!

The most amazing documentary find from the pre-Roman periods was that of a papyrus palimpsest (pl. 11b) written in a very ancient Hebrew script which palaeographically can be estimated to precede the writing on the sixth-century Lachish ostraca, and which Father Milik would put to the eighth century B.C. It is certainly an undreamed of discovery for Palestine. If this area can produce a papyrus document of such an age, what future wonders may it yet turn up from the documentarily barren period of the Hebrew kings? The superimposed text seems to be a list of names accompanied by signs, some certainly numerals. The text below is very defaced, but one can see the formula of salutation which would precede a letter.

There are a number of ostraca, nearly all inscribed in Hebrew, rarely in Greek. Many are just the letters of a name, but one large fragment of a jar (pl. 8a) bears the first part of the Hebrew alphabet, each letter being written twice. There are Greek papyri, two of them marriage contracts or the like. One is very fragmentary, but bears the word 'gift' and 'inheritance', whilst the other is better preserved and quite large, about 12 in. by 6 in. It seems to treat of the reconciliation of a divorced couple whose names are Elias and Salome. Several place names are mentioned, and the heading gives a date of the seventh year of Hadrian, i.e., A.D. 124. These and other Greek documents are all on papyrus, but some are on skin and give administrative registers, civil and military. Jewish names like Josephus, Jesus, Saulus, and Simon appear, followed by numbers and signs.

The key to the occupation of the caves during the Roman period appeared with the finding of some Hebrew letters written on papyrus and dated to the time of

the deliverance of Israel by the ministry of Simon ben Kosebah, prince of Israel.

This could be no other than the ill-fated Second Jewish Revolt of A.D. 132–5, and the person named its leader, known elsewhere as Simon ben Kochebah or Kozebah. Indeed, two of the letters were written by this person himself to the officer in charge of the Murabba'at post, a certain Joshua ben Galgula. Here is a translation of one of them:

Simon ben Kosebah to Joshua ben Galgula: greetings. I call heaven to witness against me: *if* any of the Galileans who are with you are wronged, I shall put you in fetters, as I did to Ben Aphlul.

Simon ben Kosebah ...

J. T. Milik who has edited the Semitic texts from Murabba'at suggests that 'the Galileans' are civilian refugees who have taken refuge in the villages to the south of Judaea and may have complained to the leader of the Revolt that they were being unfairly treated in the division of rations, which at this time may have been in short supply.

The main interest of the letters lies in the personality of their author and his name. The two names by which we had previously known him, Ben (or Bar) Kochebah and Ben Kozebah, mean respectively 'Son of the Star' and 'Son of the Lie', and were nicknames given him on the one hand by his supporters who regarded him as the Messiah, fulfilling the 'Star' prophecy of Numbers xxiv. 17, and on the other by his enemies who ridiculed his pretensions with this opprobrious title. Now that we see for the first time that his name was really *Kosebah*, the way in which both plays were easily possible can be understood. The 'heaven' of the opening call to witness is of course a surrogate for God, and Dr Frank Cross makes the interesting point that the call to heaven for witness is exactly paralleled by the words of St Paul in his second letter to the Corinthians, i. 23:

But I call God for a witness upon my soul, that to spare you ...

Another letter addressed to the officer in charge of the post came from Bēth Māshikô, a place presumably farther south and under Nabatean influence, to judge from the form of the name. This reads, according to Milik's rendering:

From the administrators of Bēth Māshikô, from Joshua and from El'azar, to Joshua ben Galgula, chief of the camp; greetings. Let it be known to you that the heifer which Joseph ben Ariston bought from Jacob ben Judah, who resides in Bēth Māshikô, is his by purchase. Moreover, were it not that the Gentiles are so close to us I should have gone up and made a settlement (of all outstanding claims) with you on this, that you may not say that it was out of disrespect that I have not come up to you.

Fare you and the whole house of Israel well.

> Joshua ben El'azar wrote it.
> El'azar ben Joseph wrote it.
> Jacob ben Judah, for himself.
> Saul ben El'azar, witness.
> Joseph bar Joseph, witness.
> Jacob bar Joseph, attestant.

'Were it not that the Gentiles are so close to us' tells its own pathetic story, as the Roman legions closed in on Bēth Māshikô, and it is unlikely that Joseph ben Ariston enjoyed the possession of his newly purchased heifer or indeed of anything else for very long after this letter was written.

The biblical texts from Murabba'at are, as has already been pointed out, of a strictly Massoretic character, indicating that by 132 the standardization of that tradition had most probably taken place. The most complete exemplar recovered from these caves is a scroll of the Minor Prophets which, although it has suffered considerably through damp, with a consequent blackening of the leather over large sections, on which only infra-red photography can show any writing at all, nevertheless is still recognizably a scroll. It was brought to Saad at the Museum in March 1955 by Kando who reported that some Ta'amireh Bedouin had found it shortly before. Apparently a party of five of them had discovered a tunnel entrance, overlooked during the previous searches. Inside they had noticed a stone blocking a small crevice in the cave wall, and on dislodging it with a pick had found the scroll lying concealed behind. Later investigation located the new cave about 300 yards from the grouped caves previously explored. The tunnel ran far back into the hillside, but at one point it divided into two, and the archaeologists found near by some human bones and the remains of clothing. It was near here that the scroll had been found, and it suggested that the cave had served as a sepulchre for a Jewish rebel, and, in accordance with a custom known from rabbinic writings, the biblical scroll had been buried with him.

The price asked for the scroll was reported to be something over two thousand pounds, and after a long delay the money was paid by the Museum and the scroll published seven years later.

Other small fragments found included parts of the books of Genesis, Exodus, Deuteronomy, and Isaiah, and these all are reported to have come from a confined corner of the Second Cave, and bear the marks of purposeful destruction. In particular, the fragments of Genesis xxxii–xxxv are found in a thin strip which has been torn violently across three columns of the scroll. Of a scroll of Isaiah we have only the beginning remaining, but there is one complete phylactery nearly seven inches long, written on a very fine skin whose width varies between half an inch and an inch. In a minute, semi-cursive hand, it has the three passages Exodus xiii. 1–10, 11–16, Deuteronomy xi. 13–21 in that order. A small separate piece has on it the Shema' of Deuteronomy vi. 4–9. These are the four biblical texts which the rabbis prescribe for phylacteries, and are particularly interesting in view of the 'unorthodox' phylacteries from Qumran, showing that in this as in the matter of the biblical texts themselves, the standardizing influence of the central authority had by this time made itself felt.

Another important aspect of the Murabba'at discoveries is the new and welcome light it has thrown upon the language and palaeography of second century Judaism. It will have been noticed that the letters written to the military post at Murabba'at were written in Hebrew, as were some of the contracts. This hardly accords with the oft-expressed view that long before this Hebrew had become a dead language. One can understand a dead language surviving for purely religious purposes where a conservatism in this respect lends an air of sanctity to the ritual, but letters are usually written in the spoken language of the time, and there would similarly be little point in drawing up a contract in a language foreign to its participants. We must therefore suppose that Hebrew was still being used in the first half of the second century of our era among Jews of Palestine, in a live and forceful manner which gives no sign either of being at its last gasp or of artificial resurrection for political or nationalistic ends.

The history of the cursive script of Hebrew extending over the turn of the era has been almost entirely blank for want of first-hand material. Now, thanks to Qumran, we are well equipped for the period up to 70, and from Murabba'at up to 135, but it must be admitted that the cursive Hebrew from the latter cache was so strange to our eyes that it needed deciphering like any code. Many of the letters were completely unlike anything that had ever been seen before in Hebrew palaeography, and an example which Milik finally solved was a marriage contract. Such documents are a tantalizing reminder of how little we know about the language and writing of this sparsely documented period of Judaism. Here is a translation based on that of Milik's reconstruction of the broken text according to the form of similar marriage contracts of the time:

On the seventh of Adar, in the year ele[ven of the *Governorship*, at Harodona; Judah, son of Jo . . ., son of] Manasseh of the Bene Eliashib, [resident of Harodona, has said to . . ., daughter of . . .:

Th]ou hast become my wife according to the Law of M[oses . . ., and I will give thee food and clothing from this day and for] ever and [*I will ac*]*cept* [*marital obligations towards thee, according to* . . .

I have received on thy part the dowry of thy virginity, and of money] of good coinage the sum of [two hundred] zuzin, [the equivalent of fifty tetradrachmae, and] it shall remain validly thine. In the event of di[vorce I will return to thee the money of thy dowry and all that is thine in my house. I]f thou shouldest leave for the House of Eternity [before me, the sons that thou shalt bear me will inherit the money of thy dowry with such money as may accrue to them] according to the Law. As for any daughters [thou] shalt be[ar me, they will live in my house and be maintained with my goods until their] marriage.

But if it is I who shall [depart] for this House [(of Eternity) before thee, thou shalt live . . .] and shalt receive food and clothing [continually in the house of our children for as long as] thou shalt live [. . .

All the goods that I have and] shall acquire shall stand as guarantee and [surety for thy dowry to uphold its validity] in thy favour and in the favour of thine heirs against all [contesting and claim . . .

At any time that thou shalt ask of me I will renew] for thee this document if [I am still alive.]

Judah, son of Jo [. . ., for himself.]

This contract, though badly broken, is interesting for a number of reasons, as Milik points out. The place name Harodona is probably to be identified with the modern Khirbet Haredan on the south side of the Wady en-Nar, the ancient Kidron Valley, some three miles from Jerusalem. This was possibly the home of two of David's heroes, Shammah and Elika, the *Harodites* (cp. II Samuel xxiii. 25). In the Talmud and Targums the place is mentioned as that from which the scapegoat was sent out into the desert, laden with the sins of the people, though comparison of this animal with the bridegroom is perhaps not kind. But in connexion with the scapegoat, Milik thinks that in I Enoch x. 4 the Greek name for the site where the chief of demons is cast into the pit, Doudaël, is to be amended to represent this place name.

Discoveries further South

Another batch of manuscript material was brought to the Palestine Archaeological Museum by Bedouin in the middle of July 1952, and quietly purchased by the Trustees a month later. The exact whereabouts of the source of the documents has never been officially revealed by the Museum, although it was known to be south of the Jordan border with Israel and in fact the fragments were labelled as having come from the Wady Seiyal (Nahal Seelim) about three miles north of the ancient fortress of Masada (see map on p. 8). When part of the cache was subsequently published from the Museum, the documents were said to have come from 'an unidentified location' presumably for political reasons (the Trustees included then, as now, the U.S. and British ambassadors).

Eight years later, after the truth had leaked out, Israeli archaeologists carried out their own searches in the area and set off a train of wonderful discoveries in that region of the Dead Sea. Without going into the ethics of the affair, academic and international, one cannot help feeling that a little more frankness on the part of the Trustees might have saved at least a good deal of time in the recovery of priceless antiquities which threw even more light on the history and personalities of the Second Jewish Revolt.

A full discussion of these smuggled documents must take its place in a future volume on the story of the Bar Kochebah revolt now so brilliantly illumined from recent finds on both sides of the border. An indication of the range of material found in these southern caves is that the documents included both Nabatean and Jewish papyri of business and marriage contracts and one important Greek text of the Minor Prophets on parchment. One of the contracts bears the date as of 'the third year of the Freedom of Israel', that is the last year of the Second Revolt, A.D. 135. This is how the contract reads, according to Milik's translation:

The twentieth of Iyyar, the third year of the Freedom of Israel, at Kephar-Beabyu; Hadar, son of Judah, of Kephar-Bebayu, has said to Eliazar, son of Eliazar, dwelling in the same place. I, of my own will, today have sold to you this day, my house, which communicates on the north side with my court, so that you can make it communicate with your house. And you have no claim on me in the said court. I have sold (it) to you for a sum amounting to 8 denarii, the equivalent of 2 tetradrachmae, the total price. For all time Eliazar has rights in the buying of this house, stones, beams, *furniture*, all that there is . . . ground. The limits of this house (which you) Eliazar are buying: to the East *the property of Jonathan*, to the north the court, to the west and south the (ground) purchase. And you have no claim on me in my court, and I, Hadar, may not enter or go out from this day and for ever. And I am guarantor and surety for the sale of the said house from this day and for ever.

And I, Salome, daughter of Simon, wife of the said Hadar, may raise no objections to the sale of the said house for ever more. And our present and future assets will serve you as guarantee.

This document is 'plain', and *these* have signed herein:

Hadar, son of Judah, a party, has written.
Salome, daughter of Simon, a party, has written.
Eliazar, son of Mattathiah . . .
Simon, son of Joseph, a witness.
Eliazar, son of Joseph, a witness.
Judah, son of Judah, a witness.

The place, Kephar-Bebayu, is not otherwise known (apart from a possible reference in the apocryphal book of Judith), but is probably to be located in the south of Palestine. The description of the document as 'plain' means that, unlike other papyrus contracts coming from the same source, it is not written twice on the same sheet. This convention, known otherwise from Egyptian papyri, allowed the top part, in the case of one of the marriage contracts written very small and hurriedly, to be sealed and kept in that condition until it became the subject of a legal dispute. Then the seals would be broken and only the top part taken into consideration for judging the dispute, in the case of wilful alteration of the lower copy. The signatures are on the back of the sheet, and carefully written *below* the top copy so that even when the 'original' is sealed, the names may still remain visible, presumably in case they have to be called to testify as witnesses. In actual fact, the lack of needle-holes in the papyrus of the marriage contract referred to indicates that the double copying was merely a convention and that the sealing need not at this time be carried out.

The Greek text of the Minor Prophets referred to above as found in the same cache, will have a profound effect on future Septuagint studies. The beautiful uncial writing would point to a palaeographical date towards the end of the first century of our era, which would allow of the forty or fifty years' wear till the time of the Second Revolt, which the condition of the manuscript would support. The parts of the text surviving are from Micah, Jonah, Nahum, Habakkuk, Zephaniah, and Zechariah, and these Father Barthélemy has subjected to a close scrutiny for their recensional correspondences. The results of his study are exciting and have particular reference to a work written in the second century by the great Christian apologist, Justin. This purports to be the dialogue of a controversy with the Jew Trypho, and Justin is complaining of the attitude of the Jews towards the venerable Greek tradition of the Septuagint, which they had abandoned since its adoption by the Christian Church, claiming that it was not a trustworthy basis for the claims of Christian dogmatics. This, says Justin, is unworthy of their ancestors, those seventy-two venerable scholars who performed the work of translation some four hundred years before. Furthermore, he complains that the rabbis were circulating Greek translations which were less dependable than the LXX, and goes on to give parallel examples from the old translation and the modern recensions to prove his point. It will be readily understood that, from the point of view of determining the original nature of the LXX text and how far it has been affected by later translations, Justin's book has always been of considerable interest to textual scholars. The trouble has been, however, that the earliest copy of the work extant goes back only to the fourteenth century and between then and its composition it could have suffered considerable modifications, particularly in the most important minutiae of the comparative renderings. Furthermore, the authenticity of the Dialogue itself is open to question, and even if perfectly reliable, the rabbinic Greek text Justin quotes may have been a purely local production, which could have had no effect on the general transmission of the LXX. Now, suddenly, out of the Judaean desert, this new Greek manuscript has put the matter in a new light. Barthélemy shows that the text of Justin's version agrees remarkably with this new manuscript at the hundreds of instances where comparison is possible. He shows further that this text is nothing more than a scholarly revision of the old LXX, bringing it closer to the Hebrew of the Massoretic text. In other words, Justin was perfectly correct in his arguments: the Church's Bible was not a christianizing recension specially developed by the Christian Community for dogmatic reasons, but the old Septuagint made centuries before and still being followed by the rabbinic scholars of his day. Furthermore, the rabbinic version of Aquila, long recognized as a more literal rendering of the Hebrew, and stemming from violently anti-Christian circles at the end of the first century, agrees twenty-eight times with our new text where it differs from the LXX, and shows that not only was this text also a mere revision of the LXX but that, furthermore, it was itself based on an earlier recension in the same tradition as the newly found fragments. Symmachus also, who gave a more free rendering of the Hebrew, unmarred by the pedantic literalness of Aquila, also seems to have been using our recension, for Barthélemy points out six places where, although Aquila's rendering is unknown to us, Symmachus goes with our text against the LXX. It can be shown that where he differs from our text it is simply in order to give a better Greek style.

It thus appears certain that our text enjoyed a considerable diffusion and authority in rabbinic circles of the first and second centuries. Even the Fifth Column of Origen's Hexapla, that scholar's own revision of the LXX text, seems to have been based on it, according to Barthélemy.

If this scholar is correct in his deductions, the overall effect is certainly to support the claim of the old LXX recension to a length of honourable lineage over the later, more local translations, and with the now proved fact from Qumran that it was itself a faithful rendering of a genuine Hebrew tradition, in at least the historical books, this new evidence should serve to increase still further our respect for the LXX as a reliable witness to a very early textual tradition.

Khirbet Mird

A somewhat less important, yet nevertheless interesting, cache of documentary material was uncovered in July 1952 by the indefatigable Bedouin at Khirbet Mird, two and a half miles NE. of the Mar Saba, the ancient Christian monastery not far from Bethlehem. The Arabs had burrowed into the underground chamber of a ruined monastery there, and had produced a number of Greek and Arabic papyri as well as some Christo-Palestinian Syriac works. All the documents are, of course, very much later than those coming from Qumran or Murabba'at, and date not earlier than the beginning of the Byzantine period, say, at the earliest, the fifth century, and running on till the ninth, when the monastery was destroyed. Milik has published one of the Aramaic letters, dating it approximately to the seventh century. It runs thus:

From Bless-me-my-Lord, the sinner Gabriel; to the superior of the Monastery (*laura*) of our holy father (Saba):
I beg of you that one may pray for me because of the weariness with which my heart is afflicted.
Peace be unto you from the Father, and from the Son and from the Holy Ghost.

Amen.

Biblical documents include parts of the books of Joshua, Matthew, Luke, Acts, and the letter of Paul to the Colossians, the first two and the last being hitherto quite unknown in Christo-Palestinian Aramaic. Khirbet Mird was officially excavated between February and April 1953 by a Belgian expedition under the leadership of the late Professor R. De Langhe of Louvain. They confirmed the place of origin of the fragments and found more Greek and Arabic papyri and Aramaic fragments on their own account.

THE COPPER SCROLL

As has already been said in Chapter Five, on 14 March 1952 the party investigating the cliffs behind the monastery found a cave whose roof had collapsed in antiquity. Lying close up against an inner wall were two rolled up copper strips, and scattered near by scores of leather scroll fragments and the remains of over thirty typical Qumran storage jars, more than twenty lids, two jugs and a lamp. All attempts to open the strips were frustrated by the extremely brittle nature of the oxydized metal, which simply crumbled to dust at any manipulation of the edges. This was most tantalizing since clearly visible on the outside of the rolls were Aramaic or Hebrew letters, heavily indented from the inside. Only a few words could be read through the incrustation of the copper oxide, and it was at least plain that this was no biblical document. Very gently, the strips were lifted, coated with paraffin wax, and taken to the Palestine Archaeological Museum. There they rested for three years, awaiting a solution to the problem of opening them without damaging the inscription. Reports on the chemical composition and state of the metal were sought from various quarters, and in the Johns Hopkins University of Baltimore considerable progress was made on the general problem of reconstituting corroded metals with particular reference to this matter, under the direction of Dr Corwin of that institution. These results have already proved of real worth in the archaeological field, but as far as the present problem was concerned, it was clear that the metal had completely corroded, and the chances of restoring the copper's flexibility were nil. The obvious solution was to cut the rolls into strips, thus revealing the inner surface, and provided this could be done without disintegration of the material, no harm would come to the inscription itself. There was clearly nothing of artistic value in the strips themselves, so the sacrifice of their original form could well be afforded.

The work was carried out in Manchester, England, in 1955 and 1956 (pls. 14, 15), and the full story of the operation and decipherment may be read in my *Treasure of the Copper Scroll* (Doubleday, New York, and Routledge and Kegan Paul, London, 1960). When the whole document had been cut into twenty-three strips, and its eight feet of inner face revealed for the first time, we found that it contained an inventory of buried treasure. In my opinion there is no doubt of its genuineness nor of the source of this vast wealth. Listed along with gold and silver bullion, are sacred vessels of a kind known to have been used in the Temple worship, leaving little doubt that this is the long-lost treasure of the Jerusalem Sanctuary, destroyed by Titus in A.D. 70. Previous to the final siege, apparently, the Jews in the city had wisely taken the precaution of salting away this vast wealth in predetermined hiding-places in and around the city itself, and in the deserts to the north-east and east.

One of the place-names mentioned a number of times is Secacah, found once in the Old Testament as one of the Cities of the Wilderness (Joshua xv. 61). I think we can safely identify this with Khirbet Qumran, and it is not impossible that a hoard of silver coins found under the floor of one of the rooms of the monastery (see pl. 8c) may have something to do with this treasure scroll.

The Jerusalem locations are important mainly for the light they throw on the first-century topography of the city. We may now, for instance, see for the first time in Hebrew (the language of the scroll) the name of the valley which divides the city longitudinally, the so-called Tyropoeon Valley of Josephus. 'Cheesemakers' (*turopoiōn*) has always seemed a strange name for a valley in the midst of a busy city, and in its Semitic name *gê ḥiṣônā* 'Outer Valley' we may now, I think, see how the misreading of Josephus' Greek redactors came about. There is a root *ḥwṣ* in Aramaic meaning 'to curdle' used of milk, and we may without difficulty suppose a noun *ḥiṣônā* with the meaning 'cheesemaking' with which the redactors confused the name of the valley. The description of the depression as 'outer' is perfectly natural since it ran 'outside', to the west of, the old Davidic Zion and formed its western line of defence.

There are a number of other cases where this amazing document throws new light on similar misreadings of the Semitic names given by Josephus to locations within the city. But of even greater interest is the possible information we may derive from the scroll on New Testament topography. Two items in particular warrant our attention in this regard. One speaks of a 'Tomb of Zadok', whilst the next refers to the 'Garden of Zadok'. Both the tomb and its funerary 'garden' are located by the scroll as being 'under the southern corner of the Portico'. The Portico must certainly be that called Solomon's in the New Testament and elsewhere (John x. 23, etc.), and the 'southern corner' would then be the Pinnacle of the Temple from which Jesus was tempted to cast himself down (Matthew iv. 5 etc.). Even today there can be seen a number of rock-hewn Jewish sepulchres at the foot of the Mount of Olives 'below' this point (pl. 24), and they were certainly there in Jesus' time and when our scroll was written. The reference to a 'garden' here is the only one we have outside the New Testament, and gives at least a *raison d'être* for such an enclosed area on Olivet. If the Garden of the Agony was attached, like Zadok's, to the tomb of a rich Jew, we should perhaps link Gethsemane with Golgotha and the sepulchre of Joseph of Arimathea closer geographically than the traditional and documentarily unfounded locations at present allow.

These are but a few of the interesting aspects presented by this most unexpected addition to the Qumran library. Of course, it poses very many problems, not least being how it came to be placed in Cave Three along with fragments of parchment scrolls from the Sect's library. For it is difficult to see how the Covenanters could have listed such a treasure inventory, being completely cut off from the Jerusalem hierarchy. The scroll must have come from Zealot circles, for they were masters of the city during the crucial years of preparation for the siege when this inventory was composed. They alone could have had the disposal of the sacred treasures and access to hiding places under and around the Temple. In my book I have suggested a solution to this problem, but, like so much else in the copper scroll requiring explanation, any approach can only be tentative if it is to be honest. Above all, it seems only reasonable to give its author the benefit of any doubt on his sanity, and not to dismiss the whole exciting text as the work of a fanatic, as some have done, and leave it at that. One should require far more convincing evidence than has so far been produced to see a madman's hand behind this laboriously engraved message, made at some cost on a fairly precious metal of the time, and laid carefully away with sacred scrolls from the Covenanters' library.

BIBLIOGRAPHY

1. QUMRAN MANUSCRIPTS

(a) Caves II, III, V–X

M. BAILLET, J. T. MILIK, R. DE VAUX, *Les 'Petites Grottes' de Qumran* (Discoveries in the Judaean Desert of Jordan III), Oxford, 1962 (includes Milik's version of the copper scroll).

(b) Cave III

J. M. ALLEGRO, *The Treasure of the Copper Scroll*, New York and London, 1960 (contains a complete facsimile, transliteration, translation and notes, together with detailed commentary on the text of the copper scroll, plans, maps, photographs, etc.). A later paperback edition, published by Anchor Books, New York, 1964, gives a revised translation, together with the story of an expedition to the treasure sites.

(c) Cave IV

J. M. ALLEGRO, More Isaiah Commentaries from Qumran's Fourth Cave, *Journal of Bible Literature* LXXVII, Sept. 1958.

Fragments of a Qumran Scroll of Eschatological *Midrashim*, *JBL* LXXVII, Dec. 1958.

A recently Discovered Fragment of a Commentary on Hosea from Qumran's Fourth Cave, *JBL* LXXVII, June 1959.

'An Unpublished Fragment of Essene Halakhah (4Q Ordinances)', *Journal of Semitic Studies* 1961.

'More Unpublished Pieces of a Qumran Commentary on Nahum (4QpNah)', *JSS* 1962.

' "The Wiles of the Wicked Woman": A Sapiential Work from Qumran's Fourth Cave', *Palestine Exploration Quarterly*, 1964.

'An Astrological Cryptic Document from Qumran', *JSS* 1964.

'Some Unpublished Fragments of Pseudepigraphical Literature from Qumran's Fourth Cave', *Annual of Leeds University Oriental Society*, IV 1962–3, Leiden, 1964.

Qumran Cave 4: I (4Q158–4Q186) (Discoveries in the Judaean Desert of Jordan. v), Oxford, 1968.

R. DE VAUX, J. T. MILIK and others, *Qumran Cave 4: II i Archéologie, ii Tefillin, Mezuzot et Targums (4Q128–4Q157)* (Discoveries in the Judaean Desert. v), Oxford, 1977.

BIBLIOGRAPHY

J. STARCKY, 'Un Texte Messianique Araméen de la Grotte 4 de Qumrân', *Mémoriel du Cinquantenaire de l'Ecole des Langues Orientales Enciennes de l'Institut Catholique de Paris*, 1964.

(d) *Cave XI*

J. A. SANDERS, *The Psalms Scroll of Qumrân Cave (IIQPsᵃ)* . (Discoveries in the Judaean Desert of Jordan. IV), Oxford. 1965.

J. VAN DER PLOEG and A. S. VAN DER WOUDE, *Le Targum de Job de la Grotte XI de Qumran*, Leiden, 1971.

2. MURBABA 'AT DOCUMENTS

P. BENOIT, J. T. MILIK, R. DE VAUX, *Les Grottes de Murabba'at* (Discoveries in the Judaean Desert of Jordan. II), Oxford, 1961.

II. *Selected books*

J. M. ALLEGRO, *The People of the Dead Sea Scrolls*, New York, 1958;London,1959 (complete pictorial coverage of the Scrolls story with a brief text). *The Shapira Affair*, Doubleday, W.H. Allen, 1965. *Search in the Desert*, Doubleday, 1964, W.H. Allen, 1965.

J. M ALLEGRO, *The Dead Sea Scrolls and the Christian Myth*, Westbridge, 1979.

W. H. BROWNLEE, *The Meaning of the Qumran Scrolls for the Bible*, New York, 1964.

R. DE VAUX, *L'Archaeologie et les manuscrits de la Mer Morte* (Sweich Lecture of the British Academy for 1959), London, 1961.

G. D. DRIVER, *The Judaean Scrolls*, Oxford, 1965.

J. T. MILIK, *Ten Years of Discovery in the Wilderness of Judaea*, London, 1959 (contains a useful bibliography up to that date).

Y. YADIN, *The Scroll of the War of the Sons of Light, etc.* is now translated into English, 1962.

Y. YADIN, *The Finds from the Bar-Kokhba Period in the Cave of Letters* (Judaean Desert Studies), Jerusalem, 1963.

Y. YADIN, *The Ben Sira Scroll from Masada*, Jerusalem, 1965.

3. TRANSLATIONS OF THE NON-BIBLICAL TEXTS

G. VERMES, *The Dead Sea Scrolls in English* (Pelican A551), 1962 (more literal and comprehensible than Gaster's; also more comprehensive but no translation of the copper scroll).

GENERAL INDEX

Massoretes, 6off., 64
Massoretic Text (MT), 6off.,
    63ff., 66, 74, 76ff., 158, 190
Mats, reeds, 98
Matthew, fragments from Kh.
    Mird, 191
Matthew, Gospel of, 149ff., 155
Mattock, 118
Meals, communal, 111
Meals, sacred, 131ff.
Mediator of Knowledge, 146, 167
Megiddo, 169
Melchizedek, 172
Messiah(s), 127, 131, 155, 157,
    167ff., 171ff.
Messiah of Aaron (Priestly), 131,
    164, 167, 172
Messiah, Davidic (lay, princely),
    131, 164, 168ff., 175
Messiah of Israel, 167ff.
Messianic Banquet, 113, 120,
    130ff., 164ff., 170ff.
Messianic Expectations, 45, 55,
    167ff., 175
Methusaleh, 128
Metropolitan of St Mark's, Jeru-
    salem, 20ff., 29, 32, 52
Middle Bronze Age remains from
    Murabba'at, 182
Milik, Father J. T., 53ff., 58,
    183ff., 186ff., 191
Minor Prophets, Hebrew scroll
    from Murabba'at, 185
Mird, Khirbet, 191ff.
Moab, 136
Moses, 76, 106, 154ff., 158
Moses, Song of, 74
Mount of Olives, 195
Muhammad Adh-Dhib, 17ff.,
    84ff., 97
Multitude, The, see Many
Murabba'at, 39ff., 53ff., 79, 179ff.,
    191
Mysteries, 139, 145ff., 151

Nabateau papyri from W. Seiyal,
    188

Nabateaus, 95
Nablus, 76
Nahum commentary, 105, 108,
    128
Nai, Wady en-, 187
Napthali, see Testaments of the
    Twelve Patriarchs
Nazareth, 170, 173
Nehemiah, see Ezra
Non-biblical fragments from Cave
    Four, 54
Numbers, book of, 112
Numbers, book of, fragments of,
    79

Obedas, 107
Onias III, 106
Order of Battle, see War Scroll
Origen, 63ff., 190ff.
Ostraca from Murabba'at, 183
Outer valley, 194
Ovens, see Kitchen
Overseer (Superintendent, mebag-
    ger), 99, 112, 119, 163

Palaeography, 68, 186
Palaeo-Hebrew (proto-Hebraic)
    script, 57, 76ff., 85
Palestine, 28, 41, 45, 88ff., 118,
    175, 183, 189
Palestine Archaeological Museum,
    23, 25, 28ff., 37ff., 48ff., 54,
    86, 98, 185, 187ff., 193
Palimpsest, papyrus, 183
Palm Sunday, 151
Pantry, 99, 123
Papyri: Arabic from Kh. Mird,
    191ff.; Aramaic from Kh.
    Mird, 191ff.; Greek, from
    Murabba'at, 183, 191ff.; He-
    brew from Cave Four, 54;
    Nabateau from W. Seiyal,
    188
Parables, 151ff.
Party of the Community, ('ēṣah),
    110, 119

BIBLICAL INDEX